I0555758

UP the CREEK

A compilation of seasonal essays about
outdoor life in rural Wisconsin

Ken M. Blomberg

Ten|16
PRESS

www.ten16press.com - Waukesha, WI

Up the Creek
Copyrighted © 2017, 2020 Ken M. Blomberg
ISBN 978-1-943331-47-5
Library of Congress Control Number: 2017902480
Second Edition

Up the Creek
by Ken M. Blomberg

Cover painting, "Sunset Silhouettes" © 2017 D. Bruce Prentice
Interior illustrations © 2017 D. Bruce Prentice
Cover design by Kaeley Dunteman

All Rights Reserved. Written permission must be secured from the publisher to use or reproduce any part of this book, except for brief quotations in critical reviews or articles.

For information, please contact:

www.ten16press.com
Waukesha, WI

The author has made every effort to ensure that the information within this book was accurate at the time of publication. The author does not assume and hereby disclaims any liability to any party for any loss, damage, or disruption caused by errors or omissions, whether such errors or omissions result from accident, negligence, or any other cause.

For my mother, June, who introduced me to books, and inspired me to write.

And for my wife, Lynda, and sons Erik and Karl, who share this place along the creek with me and made possible many of these essays.

FOREWORD

It's a fine spot to live, this place we call "Reality". Our home, the land and the creek lie along the Wisconsin River valley, not too far from the county line separating Portage and Marathon. The house was built before the Great Depression and our family has called it home since the late seventies. It was here that the "boss" and I raised a pair of boys, a kennel full of bird dogs and a wide variety of other critters.

The creek that flows behind the house is the lifeblood of the land. It bisects our property after draining the neighbor's woods and farm fields. Three-quarters of a mile in length, it controls the water table and eventually feeds a backwater slough that empties into the Wisconsin River. When the boys were very young, I'd dare them to spit into the creek, then ask them to imagine their saliva's journey to the ocean, by way of the Mississippi River and New Orleans.

We share our space with a variety of wildlife, including white-tailed deer, turkey, bear, fisher, grouse, woodcock, rabbit, squirrel, as well as a host of non-game song birds, owls, hawks and bald eagles. As luck would have it, it was a majestic bald eagle soaring above the river valley who convinced me to buy the fifty-year-old cheese maker's house we now call home. I contacted the realtor and closed the deal that very same day.

Over the years, our place in the country has been home to scores of bird dogs, with German Shorthaired Pointers being our breed of choice. "Buck", my first shorthair puppy, spent his initial few months living in a dormitory at the local university. He and I were kindly given an early pass to move off campus. He came to me from a small game farm near Shawano named Kentwood and taught me more about bird hunting than I could teach him about being a good bird dog. He stayed with our family for two months and fourteen days short of 16 years.

He's buried down by the creek, but his ghost still runs in the uplands behind the house. The shorthairs we own today are related to Buck, whose blood runs through their veins. The registered bloodlines of our dogs own the name of our township and a nearby river, called Eau Pleine. While many dogs from the past are buried along the creek, a new generation fills the kennel these days.

North central Wisconsin has been our home for more than three decades. Much has changed, yet a great deal is still as it was. In many respects, progress has been kind, but the consequences of development have taken a toll on the landscape. Planned growth can save the rural nature of our counties in the future, but it will take a strong land ethic, an unwavering commitment by our decision-makers and support for those who own and live on the land.

This is an ongoing story of our life, the land, the creek and the thoughts that come to mind as we share this place we call "Reality".

*****

This book is a collection of essays, divided by the seasons, largely from my weekly outdoor newspaper column *Up the Creek*, currently published by the Portage County Gazette. I thank my publisher and editor for permission to republish many of the essays and Jake Smith, Editor of the Pointing Dog Journal for the same courtesy on the essay *Puppies with No Names*.

And to relatives, friends and neighbors I mention by first names – you know who you are – thank you for your stories and inspiration.

Ken M. Blomberg
Town of Eau Pleine, Wisconsin
January 2017

CONTENTS

AUTUMN

WINTER

SPRING

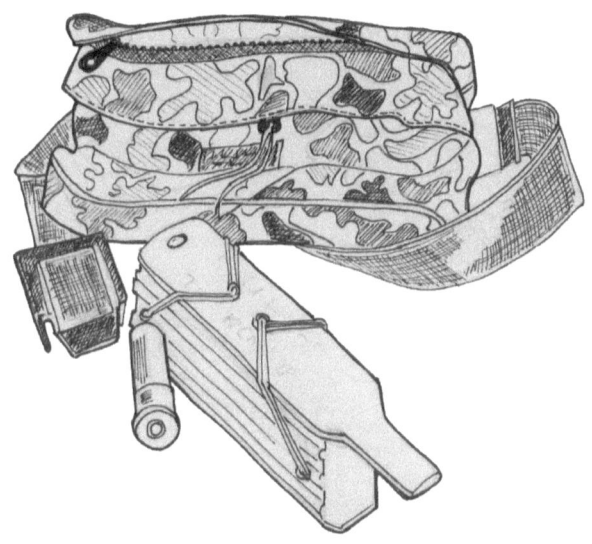

"Without spring trilliums and cattails, marsh marigolds and skunk cabbage – our piece of land would not be complete."

SKUNK CABBAGE AND TAG ALDERS

If it were not for alder and aspen, tadpoles and spring peepers, earthworms and grubs – woodcock would not return each spring to dance on our property. Without spring trilliums and cattails, marsh marigolds and skunk cabbage – our piece of land would not be complete. With old man winter still knocking at our doors, it's hard to believe that woodcock will be back in a couple of weeks.

Twenty years ago, Andy, the town assessor called a large portion of our property wasteland and it appeared exactly as that – the word wasteland on the tax roll. It was a term used interchangeably with wetlands and swamp and used to justify a lower assessment and tax. To a farm-based town, if one couldn't work the land, it was considered worthless. However, to resident woodcock, land value was measured in available food and shelter – and to that extent, they consider themselves rich indeed. You see, as the water table comes close to the surface, so too does the worm supply – a staple of their diet. Since the bill of a woodcock is only as long as a paper dollar is wide, a two-and-a-half-inch reach is the extent of its ability to grab dinner.

When the snow melts and the ground thaws out some time later this month – woodcock will return after a long journey from their southern wintering grounds – maybe as far as Louisiana. Should one or more decide to stop, then our land becomes part of their northern breeding grounds. Much to our delight and to that of our

1

bird dogs, woodcock live and dine around here for nearly seven months of the year.

Spring woodcock migration is fueled by daylight, wind and the urge to mate. Male birds actively perform their courtship "sky dance" in likely spots along the way north. Spring and fall, they feed and loaf in sheltered covers during the day and migrate after dark. Traveling at heights of somewhere around 50 feet and depending on wind direction and speed, they can cover 30 to 200 miles a day, alone, or in loose flocks – often called "flights." All along the route, male woodcock set up shop at openings in the woods – called singing grounds – next to suitable nesting habitat that attract females.

By late March, local male woodcock, most likely following the river valley, will arrive and claim one of several singing grounds on our property. They begin dancing in the sky at dusk each evening, hoping to lure any early arriving females. With a federal permit to band woodcock, my sons and I have set long, fine mist nets on the singing grounds for many years. Male birds begin "peenting" on the grounds about twenty minutes past sundown. If we're lucky, the bird gets tangled in the nets and we fasten a US Fish and Wildlife Service (USFWS) aluminum band to one of its legs. We take the appropriate measurements, including the length of its bill, which for males, measures around 66 millimeters. When we're done collecting the data, the bird is released into the darkness of the early night. Interestingly, we often hear them "peenting" even before we're done taking down the nets.

Some early spring males are migrants on their way to more northerly breeding grounds. They pick up favorable winds and continue up the Wisconsin River valley until they hit the south shore of Lake Superior, where they most likely follow a northwesterly direction to somewhere in Minnesota, or Canada. The aluminum

2

band they carry may ultimately tell their story. Local birds hang around all summer and when nesting begins around the second week of April, we keep the dogs out of the woods until the end of July. By early August, we're able to once again train our bird dogs on the adults and fully developed young of the year.

Come October, when powerful northwest winds and frosty nights return to the northern fringe of their range, woodcock begin a southerly migration. The exodus typically peaks in late October and early November, but can begin as early as September and last well into November. Autumn winds push large numbers of woodcock south. And once again, the cycle continues.

A "SKY DANCE" INSPIRATION

"The drama of the sky dance is enacted nightly on hundreds of farms, the owners of which sigh for entertainment, but harbor the illusion that it is to be sought in theaters. They live on the land, but not by the land." *

We never saw him enter the singing ground. Arriving undetected, a nasal "peent" is what gave him away. It was my seven-year-old son Erik, who heard the male woodcock first. *"Suddenly the peenting ceases and the bird flutters skyward in a series of wide spirals, emitting a musical twitter. Up and up he goes, the spirals steeper and smaller, the twittering louder and louder, until the performer is only a speck in the sky. Then, without warning, he tumbles like a crippled plane, giving voice in a soft liquid warble that a March bluebird might envy."* *

The woodcock danced for us twice before it flew into a mist net set strategically in its flight path. Together, we ran to the net from our hiding place in the brush and while I slowly untangled the bird from the nylon netting, my young son watched intently. Once freed, a small aluminum band was placed on his leg, followed by measurements of its beak and outer primary feathers. As I finished the necessary banding duties, Erik patiently waited by my side, knowing the best was yet to come. Cradled in his hands, he gently kissed the bird's forehead, pointed it away from the net and released it into the twilight.

"To band a bird is to hold a ticket in a great lottery." *

That was more than two decades ago. In the early seventies, as a freshman natural resources student at the University of Wisconsin Stevens Point (UWSP), I was introduced to "A Sand County Almanac". I didn't realize it at the time, but several of Aldo Leopold's essays were influencing my life forever.

Not one to read books from cover to cover, I skipped right to the October chapter and followed the author and his bird dog from "one red lantern to another." I learned, *"There are two kinds of hunting: ordinary hunting, and ruffed grouse hunting"* and after reflecting on his description of a good partridge dog, I was hooked.

Turning back to the Almanac's spring passages, I zeroed in on Leopold's description of the American woodcock's "Sky Dance". The essay eloquently described the courtship display, and left this reader with several unanswered questions. How long does the male display during the nesting period? Is the male's musical twitter in flight vocal, or mechanical? Are the males polygamists? If there's two birds on the singing ground, is the second a female, or a rival male? Leopold's habit of asking his readers questions, worked on me. The spell was cast.

These questions and a need to know more, led me on a lifetime love affair with the bird and the natural world it inhabited. After graduating, I began a career in water resources, free-lance writing and raising bird dogs. I joined several conservation organizations, volunteered to run woodcock singing-ground surveys and obtained my federal bird-banding license with the sole purpose of banding woodcock.

Mist netting male woodcock on their singing grounds and capturing hens and their chicks with my German Shorthaired Pointers transported me into a world few people know – and in the process, discovered the bird's world and mine weren't very

5

far apart. In the field behind our house, males and females were courting each spring. In early May, hens walked their chicks within a stone's throw of our bird dog kennels. Each fall, at dusk, birds flew above the alders bordering the edge of our woods. The sky dancer was helping me "live by the land".

One fall, a hunter in central Louisiana reported shooting a banded male mist netted near our home earlier that spring. Another was recovered in a neighbor's garden, an apparent victim of a house cat. I had banded it as a chick the previous spring a quarter mile from the garden. Several others fell to the gun in central Wisconsin. Another spring, Erik and I banded a peenting male in the field behind the house. Seven months later, it was shot near Grand Rapids, Minnesota.

On a very special weekend years ago, I visited the Leopold "Shack", made famous in the Almanac and the spell cast over me three decades ago was rekindled. The 7th Annual Leopold Education Project (LEP) National Workshop was scheduled an hour and a half travel time downstream from my home along the Wisconsin River. A Pheasants Forever web link led me to an intriguing agenda, which included presentations by nationally recognized authors, biographers and ecologists with insights into Aldo Leopold's philosophies. I was not disappointed.

I learned more than space permits from the LEP weekend workshop, but three things I must share.

My son Erik, has since earned his Masters and PhD in wildlife management and is now a professor at the University of Maine. As an undergraduate, he spent his summers trapping, banding and radio-tagging woodcock with graduate student Jed Meunier. During that LEP weekend, I learned, quite by accident, that Jed is the great-grandson of Aldo Leopold.

I also learned, that when nobody's looking, Erik still gently

6

kisses banded woodcock and other upland gamebirds farewell when released.

And finally, after more than thirty years, I learned just how much I've been inspired by Leopold's sky dancers.

*Quotes from Aldo Leopold's "A Sand County Almanac".

SPRING ARRIVES

Who among us does not rejoice with the onset of spring? Melting snow, honking geese, dabbling ducks, the first blackbird or robin – and the sweet, fresh aroma only spring air can provide. These are but a few of the early signs we've seen this week and last.

After a night's rest on the open water of DuBay, a dozen geese flew low over our house, honking with delight and telling those that would listen of picked corn and soybeans exposed on windswept fields. On Monday, the neighborhood sandhill cranes returned to the farms south and north of our place. Tuesday welcomed a small flock of robins back to our horse pasture and their white pine sanctuary. By the time this ink is dry, blackbirds and woodcock should have come home to roost.

For those of us that live in the land of four true seasons, spring has a deeper, personal meaning. It's a time to celebrate the homecoming of creatures that inhabit our woods and fields for no more than six, or seven months. That includes a host of migrant birds – their numbers too numerous to list in this space. Local resident creatures that survived winter's wrath, emerge from the recesses of deep woods and swamps – either from hibernation or solitude – and live to reproduce once more.

Suddenly, the sun stays up at the end of the day until well past seven. The extra hour of sunshine granted for energy's sake by the rascals on the east coast means little to our cardinals – whose biological clocks operate by foot-candles of sunlight, not daylight savings. The sun rises and sets at the same time each day as far as they're concerned. Despite weekly schedules and alarm clock settings, sunrise and sunset are still measured at our home by the exact time the cardinals start and end their days at the feeders.

Experts concur that a pleasant chemical reaction occurs when we're exposed to more daylight and the warmer temperatures of spring. I delight in the notion that wild creatures also feel better this time of year. As demeanors improve and spirits rise, so too does one's energy level. I suppose, that's reason enough to allow us some extra, end of the day outdoor time. Perhaps, this time, something worthwhile has trickled out of Washington.

I've watched the snow melt and the rain fall for nearly thirty-five springs along this stretch of the Wisconsin River valley. Each, and every year, with few exceptions, spring reveals much more than it leaves behind. In recent years, young sturgeons now congregate to spawn below the dam at Dubay. Black bears, rolling out of their deep winter nap, were once considered a rare sight – but are now measured as common. Canadian geese, formerly flying by on their way to northern breeding grounds, now stop and raise families on our local backwater sloughs. Gulls have colonized islands on nearby flowages and fly over the house on a regular basis. Flocks of turkeys, in numbers now surpassing the abundant deer herd, were non-existent here a few years back – as were fishers, who made their presence known during a past spring visit to our chicken coop. Eagles, seen on occasion years ago, are daily visitors to our backyard – and turkey vultures now circle the neighborhood, searching for leftovers. Bluebirds, thought by many to be the first true sign of spring, arrive on time and brighten up the neighborhood with their blue and red plumage and rich warbling whistle.

Spring has once again arrived along our creek. In town and out, it's also knocking on your back door. Take some time to soak in the extra hour of daylight the politicians so generously gave us this week. Join me in welcoming back the living things that make our neighborhoods complete.

*****

Besides all having feathers, what do swallows, vultures and woodcock have in common? All three recently came home to roost – each returning to welcoming crowds of humans, hungry for a change in seasons. All three were under the spell of vernal equinox – the first day of spring.

Each year for centuries – precisely on March 19th – citizens from San Juan Capistrano have welcomed home their beloved cliff swallows, from the bird's wintering grounds in Argentina, 7,500 miles away. Returning to the same mud nests each year, they've congregated and nested under eaves around the same old historic Mission, where two rivers converged and insects flourished. Legendary clouds of swallows have dwindled, as Capistrano has developed and food supplies have diminished. The swallows are adapting, locating further from the center of town and finding more available eaves to build their nests under. Despite it all, they continue to carry on the March 19th tradition.

Farther east, in a township called Hinkley, south of Cleveland, a nearly 200-year-old tale was repeated this year when on March 15th, buzzards returned to surrounding cliffs. Legend has it that in the early 1800s, buzzards appeared annually to feed on rotting carcasses left by area farmers. Today's Buzzard Festival is celebrated by thousands as the turkey vultures return and area merchants cash in each year on the media attention.

10

Since the early 1970's I've been keeping track of the earliest arrival date of the American woodcock, a small upland gamebird that winters as far south as Louisiana and east Texas – then migrates northward to its birthplace – in some cases right here in north central Wisconsin. Every year, give or take a week of equinox, these long-billed worm-eaters flutter into town without much fanfare. Few people know they're back, or for that matter, that they even exist. Upon arrival, they get down to business – breeding, nesting and raising families.

One past Monday, number two son and I went out back at dusk and listened for dancing woodcock. Despite snow that covered most of their singing grounds – there we found one – right on time. The sound of the male bird chirping during his descending flight gave this winter weary observer reason to cheer and marked my official annual start to spring.

What exactly is it that drives birds to migrate north each spring? Topping the list, more than anything else, is the length of daylight, or photo period. A corresponding change in the ratio of daylight to darkness. In the spring, days get longer, nights get shorter – leading up to equinox.

I do know however, that the official calendar – according to the Sun – marked yesterday, at precisely 7:07 pm, as the first day of spring. For astronomical purposes, that's the exact moment the Sun crosses directly over the Earth's equator and in the Northern Hemisphere is called the vernal equinox. On that day, the Sun spends the same amount of time above and below the horizon everywhere on Earth.

The reason we have four seasons and associated differences in the length of days is due to the 23.4-degree tilt of the Earth's axis. For those of us that live up north, the tilt positions us farther from the sun in the winter and closer in the summer. Without the tilt, day length, temperature variation and seasons would not vary. Birds would not need to migrate and weathermen would go the way of dinosaurs. Indeed, what a dull world that would be!

*****

It is official. I for one am ready for spring. You bet!

Straining for signs, I have found a few.

Here are some cases in point. Like, suddenly, the floor of our firewood shed is now visible. And the neighborhood murder of crows is restless. The small deer herd along our creek is becoming bolder by day. A chorus of male cardinals is belting out early spring love songs. River valley eagles are everywhere. Dirt can be seen peeking through snow covered farm fields. Horned larks are skirting the edges of those fields. Diving ducks are moving north on the big river's open water. And without warning, starlings have appeared at our backyard feeders.

The crows – vocal beyond the norm, seem bound and determined to broadcast their news to all that will listen. Any day now, to no surprise, they will fly by with nest building material hanging from their beaks. To their kind, February means winter roosting has worn out its welcome and it is time to break up into smaller family groups once again.

The deer, before retreating to their daytime beds, seem content to linger in broad daylight and around the pond, nibbling on the tender ends of willow brush and low-hanging branches of the weeping willow tree. Do they detect the sap that now flows, filling succulent, juicy lateral buds?

The cardinals – staking out territories and attracting their mates – announce to the world winter's upcoming demise. They surely know better than we mere mortals.

The adult eagles – neighbor Paul's bald ones, hanging around their nest these days, with laying and incubating egg duties on their minds – all the while keeping last year's young at bay. Others guard a road-killed deer carcass along the highway, even as another hangs around the big river's boat landing – talon fishing a recently thawed stretch of open water.

Early migrants to the northland, like horned larks, mark the beginning of the end of winter each year. Speckled European starlings skipped town for only a couple of months, preferring southern Wisconsin and northern Illinois in December and January. The river ducks dive for minnows wherever open water allows – moving slowly north as the ice-cover river breaks free from winter's grip.

Nothing can prevent the warming nature of the sun as it climbs higher in the sky each passing day. A month from now, when daytime temperatures rise above 50 degrees, it will behoove us to do ourselves a favor.

Take the dog for a walk to a favorite secluded spot in the neighborhood. No dog? Borrow the neighbor's. Better yet, go to the pound and adopt one. Then grab a stump or grassy knoll, sit a spell and ponder. Savor the change of seasons. Reflect on the past. Close your eyes and gaze into the future. Soak in the warmth of the sun and dream.

Tomorrow always looks better through the eyes of those that dream.

I guarantee this. Even if our wishes do not come true – it will feel good to ponder and bid welcome to spring and so long to winter – until we meet again.

WELCOMING WOOD DUCKS

Nearly thirty Aprils ago, I wrote the following words in my journal – "Was going to take a ride tonight, but decided to hang around the house. What a lucky break! Two wood ducks flew over and headed towards the woods behind the house. I kept my eye on them and what do you know? The female has a nest 200 yards from my back door in a hollow oak tree." As I recall, I cringed as she flew into the small hole at 40 miles per hour!

For years, wood ducks used that same tree cavity, until the landowner hired loggers and cut over the wooded portion of the property, including the duck's dwelling. Without older, hollow trees, the birds went elsewhere. Subsequently, our family purchased the woods behind the house, excavated two more ponds and over the years, erected six artificial nesting boxes along our creek and above the ponds. With all the right ingredients, wood ducks returned.

At one time, the wood duck was one of the most abundant waterfowl species in North America. But, by turn of the 20th century, market hunters, combined with widespread bottomland habitat destruction nearly wiped out the species. Fortunately, the Migratory Bird Treaty Act of 1918 – spearheaded by hunters and conservationists – and later coupled with the installation of artificial nesting structures, dramatically reversed the bird's demise and brought about a remarkable population recovery.

14

In 1937, employees of the U.S. Biological Survey erected hundreds of slab wood and rough-cut cypress board boxes throughout Illinois. One of those individuals was Arthur Hawkins, recognized today as a pioneer and international leader in waterfowl research and management. Art, and renowned waterfowl expert, Frank Bellrose, recognized the great management potential of the boxes and thus, helped turn the corner on the extraordinary resurgence of the species.

I had the great fortune to meet and become a friend of Art years ago, while researching an article on Aldo Leopold. I visited Art several times, who lived north of Minneapolis, on his family's wildlife refuge near Hugo, Minnesota. One of Leopold's first graduate students, Art was a wealth of knowledge regarding his famous professor and of course, wood ducks and waterfowl in general. He was a founding father of the Minnesota based Wood Duck Society and had a half dozen nesting boxes in his front yard. Sitting at his kitchen table, I heard first-hand, of the birth of wood duck nesting boxes. "The early slab wood boxes were so heavy," he said, "that we had to use a crane to hoist them high enough up into the trees." They soon realized a lighter version would be more practical. Art passed away at age 92, while hiking at his refuge, looking for spring migrants – walking stick and binoculars in hand.

Described by many as the most beautiful of all waterfowl, the male wood duck – in its fall and winter multi-colored plumage – sports a green head with white stripes along the face and crest, a white throat patch, chestnut breast, golden flanks and white belly. But it's the iridescent dark green-blue back and wings, as well as his red bill and eyes that draw attention.

Each year in late March, or early April, wood ducks return to this stretch of the Wisconsin River valley to nest and rear their young. The hens lay between 9 and 14 eggs and the day after they hatch in May, the baby ducklings use their sharp claws to climb to the nest entrance and then jump to the ground. The tiny ducks can tumble from great heights without injury and make their way to water where they immediately swim and find their own food.

Three decades ago, I watched a female wood duck fly full speed into a hole in an old oak tree behind the house. These days we watch in anticipation as another generation uses the nesting boxes we have placed in the woods out back. Last week I checked all the boxes, cleaning out old material and adding new sawdust as bedding. One box already contained five eggs, with no sign of the female. Eggs are laid a few at a time – so it may be a week before she begins incubation full time. Then we'll be watching and if we're lucky, we'll see what few people ever witness – baby ducks leaving the nest.

SPRING WALKS

With only a month left before a regularly scheduled physical with our family doctor, I decided to get off my "you-know-what" and start a regular daily habit of strolling around the field behind the house. When related to exercise and a healthier lifestyle, walks out back take on new meaning. The "boss", who'd rather go longer and faster – bless her heart – puts up with my slower velocity. Each evening, with binoculars and camera around our necks, off we go.

Years ago, a learned forestry professor taught me how to determine the length of my pace. Every two steps became 5.6 feet – and I've been counting ever since. A hundred-yard target for sighting-in my deer rifle translated into 53 and a half paces. My longest shot dropped a deer in its tracks at a hundred and forty-two paces, or 265 yards. The distance between my septic system and well is 28 paces. Who needs a tape measure when a good pair of hiking boots will do just fine?

Out back, once around the horn is about a half mile – two times equals a mile – three makes a mile and a half – well, you get the idea. By working my way up to four laps before doctor-day, I might just get the nerve to look Doctor Dean square in the eyes and tell him I'm getting plenty of exercise. And if I lose a few pounds in the process, it might appear I didn't gain too much weight over the long winter months. If none of that works, perhaps changing the subject and talking about the upcoming fishing season might – or better yet, any trout fishing excursions he may have planned. With luck, he'll suddenly realize he's got real sick folks to tend to and I'll sneak out with a nothing more than a warning.

If one measures each revolution of the field in miles per hour, or calories per minute, the value calculated by things we see and hear while walking is missed. Like the Bald Eagle that flew above the east fence line last Monday night. Or, on Tuesday, the pair of wood ducks that swooped towards one of the ponds in the woods – just minutes before a pair of Canada geese flew over the horse pasture. Each night, bluebirds play hop-scotch from one common Mullen stalk to another and one evening, while the pileated woodpecker cried out from deep in the woods, our dog Mossy, watched intently as a killdeer flew across the neighbor's disked soybean field.

We try to take a different dog along each night – the freedom they enjoy away from their kennel run is especially noticeable in the spring, as they shake off the winter doldrums. Now that the nesting season upon us, we're careful to keep them under control and on a lead. After all, the resident female woodcock are surely on their eggs by now – and by the first of May we'll be banding chicks.

A walk around the field is also a time to ponder. Where exactly should I plant the wildlife packet we ordered from the Griffith state nursery? Is it time to burn, graze, or mow the prairie grass this year? Do I have time to hang one more wood duck house this spring? Is the deer trail bisecting the field exactly where it was last spring, or has it shifted a bit to the west? Where's the best spot for a purple martin house?

If walking, and observing and pondering is good for one's health and well-being, then our evening strolls are a good thing. It's a habit the boss and Doc will no doubt encourage – and goodness knows, my list of habits could stand to gain at least one good one!

18

A RARE GUEST

The field out back of our home in the country is part prairie grass, part food plot – has a small pond and is surrounded by woods and cropland. It has attracted a wide variety of wildlife over the years – including a long list of native mammals and birds found in our family's collection of field guides. This past weekend, an unexpected migrant visitor stopped by and took us by complete surprise.

It was the pond that attracted our unusual guest. Vera's Pond, named after my late Aunt from Arizona, is man-made, but in reality, is neighbor Cliff-made. It covers less than an acre – but for us, is measured in entertainment per square foot. While it's mainly a breeding hole for frogs, it can be home for an occasional wood duck, merganser, mallard, teal or Canadian goose – it's even lured in a rare eagle, or osprey eye-balling our pond's bluegill, crappie and perch. A small patch of cattails on the north end of the pond housed a red-winged blackbird's nest last year and the flying insects that emerge from the water's surface act like magnets to swooping swallows. Neighborhood morning doves, raccoons, deer and turkeys call it home when thirst drives their movements. Over the years, a regular cast of characters have occupied this center stage of the field.

So, you can imagine my amazement – while filling the upstairs bird feeder and enjoying a Sunday morning cup of coffee – that I would hear the unmistakable haunting laughter of a Common

Loon coming from the direction of the pond. I about spilled the bird seed and coffee while focusing on what I had just heard. Had it just flown by? After all, loons do call while in flight. But no, a few minutes later the loon repeated its call from the exact same location.

According to field guide books, the loon has four calls, the hoot, wail, tremolo and yodel. The one-syllable "hoot" is used to keep in contact. The "wail", most often used at night, sounds more like a wolf howl than anything else – is also meant to keep tabs on others. When a loon "yodels", you can bet it's a male and he's defending his territory. The one I heard out back was the "tremolo" call – which signals alarm or irritation. Had the noise from our deck door, or me stumbling in the morning stillness startled the bird?

A few years back, after noting a breeding pair of loons at the Mead Wildlife Area, I signed up for the Sigurd Olson Institute LoonWatch program. This organization promotes loon education and coordinates a volunteer loon monitoring program on Wisconsin lakes from spring to fall. They record loon activity like annual arrival and departure dates and nesting success. Every five years, since 1985, they have conducted the Wisconsin Loon Population Survey – a one-day survey that tracks population trends of our state's loons. It's indeed an amazing bird. They're considered to be among the oldest group of birds alive today – their history stretching back more than 50 million years. Huge in size, compared to most waterfowl, their wingspan stretches 42 to 58 inches and they can weigh up to 14 pounds. They mate for life and return to the same lake and territory during breeding season. While feeding, they can dive underwater for about a minute.

That weekend, loons were a common sight up and down the river valley. When I sent in my loon arrival field data form to LoonWatch in Ashland, I noted observing four pairs on the Wisconsin River and Lake Dubay. The fishing is good, so they should stick around for a week, or more. Grab your binoculars and take a drive up, or down the river and look for loons. And while you're at it, look for diver ducks – like mergansers, goldeneyes, scaup and buffleheads – they are everywhere.

As a final gesture, our temporary guest did a fly-by across the field and headed north – no doubt for breakfast on Dubay. And luckily for us, its brief visit will survive in our memories for years.

A PAIR OF TURKEY HUNTS

Number two son and I became hunters of turkeys last week. We traveled downstream an hour and a half to where long ago, glaciers stopped and today, hills and valleys stand tall and wide. It was there, at a friend's horse farm, that we set up our base camp. We'd enter the woods each morning before daybreak, pause for late morning breakfast and hunt until sunset. We dressed in camouflage, walked for miles and conversed with turkeys for hours. And at night, we slept the deep sleep only hunters understand.

At the end of the first day, our host had lured a mature twenty-pound tom turkey to his hen decoy on the hilltop behind his house. Jimmy hunts only two things – deer and turkey – and he does both extremely well. At the time, he built Mathews compound bows for hunters in Sparta. He took us under his wing many years ago, and shaped us into respectable turkey hunters.

To enter the woods and hunt these big birds is to journey into a world like no other. Enthusiastic male turkeys shake the quiet spring mornings with their heart-stopping, treetop calls. When they explode with deep-throated gobbles, others of their kind follow suit. Before long, the valley is on fire, as the infectious gobbling causes birds up and down the ridge line to join in the chorus. At that moment, hunters know it's time to imitate a lovelorn hen with a yelp or two. We call out and they gobble back. They gobble and we call back. Leaning over their perch, high atop the tree line, they stretch their necks as far as they can reach and call out once more. After this back and forth exchange, which can last for up to a half an hour or more, they make a move and fly down off their perch – hopefully in the direction of our call and the hen decoy we've strategically placed away from our blind.

The wild turkey has been admired by many over the years, and at times, exalted by the famous. Like Benjamin Franklin, who said, "I wish the Bald Eagle had not been chosen as the representative of our country. He is a bird of bad moral character. He does not get his living honestly...the turkey is in comparison a much more respectable bird, and withal a true original native of America...He is besides, tho' a little vain and silly, a bird of courage."

It's true they're noble birds, dressed in cloaks of bravery and audacious when it comes down to courting the opposite sex, but at times, they turn into downright fools – as evident when they become hell-bent on sharing the dinner table with a bowl of cranberries and stuffing.

That was the case on the second day, when number two son and I shared the pre-dawn darkness and a ridge top with at least six gobblers. One pair headed towards Karl, another duo came my direction, where I hid on a rocky point. At a quarter past six, the dominant "king" tom of the ridge, overcome by lust and fooled by a slate call and foam rubber hen decoy, met his match in my son. A shot, heard round the valley, sent the king tumbling down a steep hillside and into the record book.

At the shot, the turkeys near my hideout, like me, remained frozen in place. As I slowly reached for my call, the younger jake noticed movement and in the blink of an eye, they disappeared over a rise in the field and into the woods beyond. So goes turkey hunting. Just as well, as it was time for handshakes and pictures. Working my way slowly along the ridge, I paused from time to time to soak in the grandeur of this turkey kingdom. An unusual stillness hung over the valley. Normally windswept, the hillside was now an amphitheater for other creatures, like several varieties of woodpeckers, nuthatches, chickadees, robins and cardinals. Down in the valley, a rooster ring-necked pheasant crowed out, announcing his possessions to the world.

Later, on the scale at the check station, Karl's bird weighed in at 28 pounds, the heaviest registered to-date at our hunting camp. The youngest of our crew suddenly became the center of attention, a well-deserved distinction. On that day, at the Lone Star Café, where turkeys are registered and hunters gather, the eggs, sausage, potatoes and toast tasted better, the coffee aroma emerged richer and the talk around the table turned out to be more electrifying. So goes turkey hunting.

*****

Hunting can be a complicated, solemn affair. Or, it can be a simple, beautiful and relaxing experience – where everything seems to fall exactly into place. Hunting in the fall involves a lot of planning, preparation and commitment. But a spring hunt for turkey can be a thing of splendor – with flowers on the landscape and music in the air. That was the case when round two of this year's turkey hunt took place for us during the sixth, and final season.

The recipe for our gourmet turkey hunt included the following ingredients; favorable weather, co-operative birds and more than generous neighboring landowners who granted access to their land. In the end, magically, it all came together in time and space. If our hunt could be compared to a song, it played out like a symphony.

The adventure began when number one son cashed in a free,

overbooked airplane ticket – flew into central Wisconsin from school out east and joined his younger brother and the "old man" to hunt turkeys. The first day began well before dawn, as number one and I snuck into the woods behind the house. Nestled in a ground blind, we listened as the creatures of the forest awoke, one at a time. An hour elapsed without indication from our quarry – despite my son's expert hen turkey calling, the screech of an owl and several raucous crows – all of which normally evoke responses from any nearby gobblers. It was time to move.

Within a half hour of relocating our operation to a neighboring "40", several hens and a lone tom turkey were lured towards our blind with well-placed decoys and premeditated calling. An accomplished wildlife photographer, number one was so busy snapping pictures of the displaying tom, he nearly forgot to pick up his gun. But in the end, he traded "weapons" and our first bird was on its way to the freezer.

After returning from town and the registration station, it was the "old man's" turn. With a hen feeding in a clover patch near the blind and a tom displaying across an adjacent plowed field, we were forced to sneak into the blind from a wooded area. Before we had a chance to call in the tom, a rather strong storm cell descended and dropped some significant rain, while nearly blowing over the blind. By the time the precipitation subsided, the 4:30 am wake-up call had caught up and unconsciously, I nodded off for a few minutes. My eyes opened and there he was – twenty yards away – appearing quietly as a ghost. He came in silently, looking for the hen my son had cleverly fabricated with slate and striker. He left the scene slung over my right shoulder.

The second day of our hunt brought number two son into the picture, as he completed his college finals and was ready to hunt. The boys decided to try a place on River Road, where neighbor

25

Paul had pointed the way. Up before dawn once again, they set up under several roosting gobblers, placing decoys in the field and waiting for them to fly down. Number one remarked that with very little encouragement, a single tom raced across the field, like "he was on a rope and we were pulling him in."

This late-season hunt was about more than harvesting turkeys. For this scribe, it was counting warblers, walking with sandhill cranes, a post-hunt breakfast of scrambled eggs and turkey tenderloin, a marinated turkey shish kabob dinner at a weekend family get-together – and more than anything, spending quality time with both sons, now grown men that have all but left the home nest. It was a perfect hunt, with all the right ingredients – one where everything fell exactly into the right place.

A RIVER FLOAT

Weekends come and go way too fast. But when time off from work arrives, like the rest of you, our family tries to make the best of every minute. That was certainly the case that weekend. A boat ride, birthday celebration, tree planting, visitors and building benches filled a good portion of our plate for two days.

A float down the river is a lazy way to spend an afternoon and unless you're in a hurry, it's a grand way to blend together one's mind and body. That's the way it was for me on opening day of the fishing season last Saturday – a three-and-a-half-hour drift down a few miles of the Wisconsin River. My craft was a ten-foot Jon boat – one I purchased as a teenager nearly forty years ago – a vessel that has taken me on many adventures over the years. Besides the Wisconsin, we have traveled as one down rivers like the Fox, the Mississippi, the Rock and the Chippewa. As far as lakes go, there's just too many to list.

My weekend journey began at the dam below the Dubay flowage and ended near the slough that takes water from our creek. A handful of fishermen were working the waters below the dam, taking an occasional fish or two as I passed by. The Wisconsin is a walleye factory and its waters contain most species of fish known to exist in our state – including of late, an impressive showing of sturgeon and catfish. More recently, much to the surprise and dismay of fish managers, white bass have taken hold above the dam.

27

Did you know our state was named after this inspiring river? The largest and longest river in our state, it stretches nearly 430 miles and passes through the heart of many communities – all owing their existence to the watercourse itself. While my journey just scratched the surface, it followed a large portion of the eastern edge of our township. On the map and as the crow flies, my trip covered less than four miles. Crisscrossing from bank to bank, like a bird dog searching a woodlot for a partridge, my final mileage was a bit longer. Meandering allowed me to explore a few backwater sloughs and observe some feathered residents of the waterway. A pair of islands, downstream from the dam insisted that I pay them a visit and it was there that a half dozen spotted sandpipers put on quite a show. Several pair of belted kingfishers greeted me with reservations as I floated past their deep burrows in the steep, high banks near Deer Island. Their loud, harsh clatter sounded a warning – perhaps as I approached too closely to their nests. They went back to fishing, diving repeatedly head-first into the water. Maybe they were busy gathering food for their newly hatched young – who were waiting up to eight feet deep in their bank side nests.

I rowed across the river, only to interrupt an immature bald eagle, who was also fishing – sending it on its way south, where it met up with a pair of white-headed adults, no doubt the parents. Their nest, a half-mile west, and the dam, a half mile north, keep the family in the neighborhood year-round. Hunting will intensify as this year's young get older and hungrier. Occasionally, they'll fly over our place on the creek and perhaps, as in the past, may snatch a fish from one of our ponds.

A backwater slough held wood ducks, mallards and a great blue heron, which rounded out the short checklist of birds spotted that day. With the wind at my face, I rowed past a dead tree, hollowed out by time and woodpeckers. Something white caught my eye in a hole towards the top. A sun bleach skull of a raccoon rested in the opening, as if the furbearer had fallen asleep while gazing over its beloved river bottom. Faded fur peeked over its back, revealing an identity, I snapped some pictures while floating by – and contemplated the story behind the animal's demise – then named that spot forever in my mind "coon skull point".

My river float ended, but not the weekend. Day two was my birthday. With no plans or expectations, the day blossomed like the new trilliums in the woods. From waking up to a phone call from number one son, who's attending graduate school out east, to the secret plans the boss had in store for me – a perfect day evolved. Number two son and his girlfriend arrived and spent the day – building Leopold benches and planting three hundred wildlife shrubs along a new fencerow. Steaks on the grill and neighbors stopping by for a chat, rounded out a great weekend that began with a simple, old fashioned float down a lazy river – reliving the distant memory of a much younger boy and his faithful Jon boat.

WATCHING BIRDS

The more I learn about birds, the more I discover how little I know.

Over the years, bird watching has become a favorite pastime for our family. The boss calls the feeders and the birds that frequent them hers and seems to revel in the fact that over time, her kitchen has become a gathering place for family and guests – drawn to the kitchen table like chickadees to the sunflower seeds. The table is pressed up against the picture window that overlooks the feeders and any given time, a spotting scope, binoculars and bird books can be found sharing the table with dishes and silverware.

Number one son, while scouting along River Road, found good numbers of migrant warblers in a young growth aspen stand – including, Yellow Warbler, Common Yellowthroat, Golden-winged Warbler, Chestnut-sided Warbler, and American Redstart. Later in the day, together, we were able to practice calling by "kissing and spishing" several varieties into the open. By kissing and squeaking the back of our hands where the thumb and forefinger meet, or by simply making a long, drawn-out "spish-h-h-h" sound several times in a row – one can draw songbirds out of hiding. Some say the sound resembles an alarm call and other birds simply respond by coming in to help. Like many of you, I – a late bird watching bloomer – have a personal "life list" of birds that I've spotted and identified over the years. With more than forty varieties of warblers known to swing through, or reside in our state each year, reaching out and searching past the limited confines of our creek bottom is in order. My personal list is long overdue for an update and needs a jumpstart if I ever hope to complete seeing all bird varieties that call Wisconsin home, or a stop-over in their migration travels. A "life list" is just the ticket for that journey.

*****

The alarm went off at 2:30 am. My eyes opened five minutes later, after rolling out of bed and getting dressed in the dark. I stumbled downstairs, made a small pot of coffee and let the dogs out the back door. In the process, I woke up my mother, who slept on the living room couch, dressed and ready to go. At eighty-four-years old, she continues to meet this annual pilgrimage with the enthusiasm of a veteran deer hunter. You see, for the past quarter of a century, religiously, she and I have repeated an annual Memorial Day weekend tradition of counting Mourning Doves.

With the dogs back in the house, traveling coffee mugs in hand and on the road by 3:15 am, we traveled downstream an hour and fifteen minutes to the starting point of a Mourning Dove Call-count Survey for the U.S. Fish and Wildlife Service – Route Number 0910 – a path that stretches 20 miles between Waushara and Green Counties. Parked alongside a state highway, thirty-minutes before sunrise, we had time to reflect on dove counts from the past. After all, the year 2007 marked a milestone of sorts for both of us – twenty-five years of consecutive surveys.

Route 0910 starts and ends on land that supports farming, but its core runs through the White River State Wildlife Area. Along the way, State Rustic Road R22, becomes our pathway as we slice a piece of dynamic public domain in half, counting doves along the way. The first stop begins precisely at thirty-minutes before sunrise and like the nineteen that follow, allow exactly three minutes to count all individual doves heard "cooing". Then it's into the car and on to the next stop, exactly one mile down the road. At each stop, the number of birds heard calling are recorded, as well as those seen while stopped – and driving between stops, the number of birds observed along the way are also noted.

Designated stops, numbered for statistical purposes, take on their own personality and over the years, have been given nicknames. Like number 6, the "sunrise stop". Every year, at exactly 5:21 am, clouds willing, we're treated to spectacular daybreaks. One year number one son tagged along and we discovered a beaver lodge right on the edge of the gravel road at stop number 18, the "beaver lodge stop". Curiosity got the better of grandma and number one as they stood on the doorstep of the lodge. They leaned closer and closer, until they heard the cries of newborn baby beaver "kits" – their whining noises filtering from a nest of branches and sticks. Then there's the "red fox stop", number 20 – the "lupine stop", number 10 – the "baby raccoon stop", number 15 – and new this year, the "turkey roost stop", number 11. Number two son's favorite is a post survey stop, the "Sunshine Restaurant stop". There are other names, but you get the idea. Each stop on the route has its own personality and charm – yearly homecomings, one and all.

The annual Mourning Dove Call-count Survey provides the USFWS an index to population size as well as data for determining long-term population trends. The mourning dove (*Zenaida macroura*) is one of the most plentiful and widely dispersed birds in North America – with an estimated fall population of from 350 to 600 million birds – while at the same time, biologists predict that 4-5 million doves migrate from our state each fall. Surveys have been conducted annually since 1953, and encompass more than 1,000 routes across the U.S., including approximately twenty-two in Wisconsin. Since 1983, mother and I have monitored Route 0910 – and from a low of 19 birds heard and 12 viewed in 1997, to a high this year of 75 heard and 39 seen – our adopted route has averaged just over 49 birds heard and 18 observed each year. 2007 will go down in the books as a record banner year!

Next year, my devoted partner and I will wake up well before dawn, gather our clipboard, checklist, pencil and coffee mugs and continue this labor of love. Our contribution is but a small piece of a much larger puzzle – that of keeping tabs on the status of Mourning Doves here and across the country. And who knows? Maybe the numbers will increase again next year and a new record will be set on Route 0910.

*****

I believe it was humorist Will Rogers who once professed, "I love a dog. He does nothing for political reasons."

Perhaps, in the same vane, that is why I like all things wild and free – as they do nothing for political justification. Unless, of course, you consider the daily show right outside the kitchen window – an event I submit to you as birdfeeder politics. Even an untutored eye will notice the backyard bird chain of command, on display for those willing to observe.

On top of the ladder is the governing shrike – appearing now and then – but for the most part hiding in the shadows. When he enters the picture, all others scatter – bowing to his stature and position on top of the food chain. At his side, are the lieutenant governor, attorney general and secretary of state – Blue Jays, one and all.

Our senate of cardinals come and go as they please, but are first to arrive in the morning and last to leave at the end of the day. A mixed caucus of chickadees, juncos, redpolls and finches make up our assembly and can be found here, there and anywhere – quick to debate any birdseed deficit, swift to seek subsidy offerings. Their legislative support staff – nuthatches and sparrows, dig in and clean up after those higher on the feeder's organizational chart. No matter what issues come to the plate, at the end of the day, all the political players at the feeder retreat and roost to survive the elements of the night.

Daylight each morning brings lobbying woodpeckers of various legal stripes, which can be caught roaming the box elder and locust halls, beaks open for leftover pork and fat scraps at the trough. Always on top of their game, they are at their best while entertaining feeder landlords, influencing bureaucratic birdwatchers and securing passage of suet legislation.

Bi-partisan at times, but for the most part, split by party – peace-loving doves on the left and more aggressive hawks circling the sky to the right. That is, until election storms roll in. Then it's every bird for himself. Low pressure fronts trigger feeding frenzies, while feathered candidates perch above them all, singing promises of better weather, full feeders and sunny skies.

Will Rogers, a political satirist and friend of presidents, senators, prime ministers and kings, loved to poke fun at elected officials from all parties. He knew the nature of their antics and enjoyed following the affairs of state and nation.

He summed it up when he quipped, "Politics is the best show in America. I love animals and I love politicians and I love to watch both of 'em play..."

CLEAR CUTTING PAYS OFF

The maple tree was merely twenty years old, but it had to come down – but not before several small ironwoods in the way were toppled. Thirty feet to the north, a white pine was spared, but birch and popple, fore and aft were slain. A very young hemlock was given a pass.

No. 2 son took the chainsaw to the maple, notching the base before delivering the final blow. I stood to the side and pushed. Before the top hit the ground, we noticed sap flowing from the cut like blood from a severed artery. Tree after tree must be downed – out with the old, in with the new. So, it goes, when woodlands must be managed for young forest wildlife.

The scene was bittersweet, as this marked the first clear-cut on our property since the land became ours in title. The previous owner hired loggers in the late 1980s to harvest everything over 8 inches in diameter. Stumps from that cutting remain as testament to an old-aged forest that dated back to the original logging era of the late 1800s. Before railroads, lumbermen first cleared the forests – including ours – to within just a few miles of the Wisconsin River.

Clear-cuts are defined by some as a controversial harvest practice in which most or all trees are cut down. In that case, the words invoke fear and distain. In my circle, the term rests secure, as we know – at least in the Great Lakes region – clear-cutting restores the health of the land by providing young-aged forests that are critical to the well-being of warblers, woodcock and hundreds of other feathered and furred creatures.

According to those in the know, like biologists of the Ruffed Grouse Society (RGS), "Many songbirds, including the golden-winged warbler, chestnut-sided warbler and field sparrow, are more abundant in young aspen stands than in other forest habitats. But their numbers are declining throughout eastern North America, along with those of ruffed grouse and woodcock, as our aspen forests mature and leave a scarcity of young, dense forests."

Our cut, the first of series of four planned south of the house will cover no more than 2 acres each. Clear-cutting allows species that regenerate from the root systems, which are left intact underground. Daylight of high intensity in the newly disturbed open areas encourages new growth to spring forth from shallow root systems. Planned clear-cutting removes nearly all trees in a given area.

In the grand scheme of things, our small clear-cut on the back 40 is rather insignificant. But to a handful of birds and mammals that call young forests home, it may become the center of their world.

And the firewood created from the downed birch, popple and maple will warm our home next winter.

SEASON OF IN-BETWEENS

'Tis the season of in-betweens.

Fishermen pass by our home, pulling their boats on trailers in search of walleyes below the dam, while ice fishermen soak minnows for the same on still frozen backwater sloughs. One boat was spotted on the main river channel, while three brave souls fished on the ice, in-between the boat and the shore.

Snow still covers the forest floor; even as bare fields emerge in preparation for spring.

Neighbors and friends are now tending their maple syrup sugar bushes – from our own township all the way to Park Falls and places in-between. Sap runs best this time of the year, in-between warm days and cold nights.

And wildlife, some here and others there – in-between – some ready to return home, others just waiting for spring.

On Saturday, the boss and I traveled downstream to the land of Christmas trees and crystal clear waters to visit her folks and pick up a load of firewood. In the process, we heard the trumpets of the first returning sandhill cranes of the season – just south of Wautoma – then watched as they swooped from the sky and landed on a field near the farm we were visiting.

After No. 2 son and I unloaded the firewood on Sunday, I climbed aboard my tractor to check trail access for next weekend's family woodcutting gathering. Friends that tend farms have known for a long time that the best place to view wildlife up close is from the seat of a tractor. That's the way it was for me that day.

Along the trails that interlace our land, I happened upon a trio of bedded deer at twenty yards. In unison, their heads swiveled right to left as I passed by in low gear. Ten minutes later, upon my return, they were still there. And once again, at a snail's pace, their heads pivoted – this time left to right as I passed on by.

A flock of turkeys occupying our horse pasture were not so patient, but obligingly flew out of the white pines and over the neighbor's picked cornfield – one at a time, exactly twenty-seven times.

Then, while eyeing up some mature maples suitable for harvest, I spotted a hen ruffed grouse at the base of a balsam, soaking up the sun – frozen like a statue. Like the deer, she stood her ground and was right there on my return loop, a half hour later. Unlike the deer, her head never moved. I stopped and took a good look, and at twenty feet her short tail gave her gender away. I wondered – do female grouse have more patience than their male counterparts? On Monday, the first of our neighborhood sandhill cranes returned – their lonesome cries music to my ears.

And a few weeks from now, maybe sooner, the snow will be all but gone. The creek will flow strong when the surrounding landscape drains surplus groundwater, rainfall and what's left of melting snow.

Spring is knocking at our door as we find ourselves in-between seasons.

SUMMER

"I watched as he stood high on top of a car sized boulder – my son, no longer boy, but a man of talent, handling life as skillfully as he handles a fly rod."

PUPPIES WITH NO NAMES

Where do puppies with no names go when they die? That question crossed the old man's mind as he drove the off-road utility vehicle towards the woods.

The answer was beyond his reach – yet the question persisted. As he passed through the prairie grass field and approached the pond, he spotted a doe grazing in a food plot. He pondered the whereabouts of any fawns. After all, it was the first week of June and one or two must be hidden nearby in the tall grass on the edge of the woods. The doe looked up, paid him no mind and returned to her morning meal.

The old man moved on, pausing for a moment near a cattail pond. A clearing at that point let the sun shine in and warmed anything in its path. He shut off the engine, leaned back and soaked in the heat. Again, he contemplated, "Where do puppies with no names go?"

Earlier that morning, after showering, he combed his hair. There, gazing back, was an old man. The aging process had really caught him off guard. Wrinkles, gray hair and worry lines replaced middle age. Where have all the years gone? Staring him in the face was a good dose of reality. An unpleasant job was at hand and it reflected in his face.

At this stage in life he had come to realize certain realities are self-evident. And after more than 40 years of raising gun dogs he recognized not all pregnancies and deliveries go smoothly.

43

Sometimes there are complications. Sometimes puppies die early on. If people only knew, he pondered. Luckily, these mishaps are exceptions, not the rule. On occasion, puppies die before given a name.

Most folks are greeted by a whelping box full of lively, rambunctious pups the day they come to make their pick. Fortunately, the occasional losses occur early on. New owners are shielded – as they should be. They leave with a decade or more of joy and happiness in their arms. Breeders like the old man share in that pleasure. That in itself makes up for the pain of occasional losses. Puppies with no names disappear like the wind. Or do they?

The trail he followed that day ended at the highest point on his property. It was a place he had buried puppies with no names in the past. Puppies with no future. Puppies that would never hear, see or smell – never put a smile on a child's face, or cuddle with their littermates.

The old man put the two stillborn and one born too small and weak to survive together in a coffee can, snug and together – not unlike while in their mother's womb. He dug a hole and buried them on the "hill" – not far from an old ruffed grouse drumming log and next to a large white pine that served the old man well as a backstop during the recent spring turkey hunt.

He wiped the sweat from his brow and a single tear that found his cheek. Suddenly he recalled a moment 30 years past. A visit from his parents shortly after a litter of puppies was born. A large litter – 13 if he recalled correctly – but 2 died shortly after birth. He had already buried them on the hill and grumbled to his father, "What a waste."

His father was a gentle, wise man with nothing but good things to share. He wore an old man's hat that covered a balding head. "Maybe it is God's way," he said. "For every puppy that

44

dies, there's a baby waiting in Heaven. There they both grow older together waiting for the rest of us."

The old man returned to his ride and loaded the shovel. But before departing, looked to the sky, smiled and whispered, "Thanks Dad."

GRAVEL ROADS

I remember walking into his office and taking a seat, all the while gazing at maps on the walls and books on the shelves. County Sanitarian Bob knew the township well and wondered out-loud, "Ken, why in the world would you want to buy a house in that area? It's plagued with high groundwater and bedrock and most of the septic systems are failing."

"That's exactly why I want to live there." I replied. "Less chance of other houses being built close by and that is the way I'd like it to stay."

Thirty years later – guess what? I was right.

Three decades ago, within one square mile of our home, only five other occupied dwellings existed. Today, that number is six.

According to county records, the population of our township peaked out in 1920 at 1,126, then dipped to a low of 784 in 1970 and has slowly grown over the years to its current level of about 960.

In 1928, a home and cheese factory was built on the land we now occupy. It was a focal point for the immediate area and neighbor Cliff remembers fondly of stopping occasionally for cheese, or ice cream while in route to the one-room school house on Maple Road.

Both buildings still stand today – we reside in a house the cheese-maker built and that we later remodeled – and store our "stuff" in the retired brick factory across the street. A gravel road runs between the two structures – neither one meeting modern road setbacks – but the distance makes for some cozy "howdy-dos" to passer-bys and neighbors while we sit on the front deck.

Our community has seen a rather controlled growth rate as of late. We have watched as family dairy farms dwindled, old timers passed on and youngsters moved to town – at the same time as available land along the waterways was split and settled by newcomers. Even as river and lake frontage became sliced up and developed, farmland, for the most part, remains intact. The town planning committee has turned back attempts to subdivide farmland, instead leaning towards future small cluster development, with most forties remaining untouched.

Recently, however, something of note fell below my radar screen. Perhaps it happened at this year's annual town meeting, or at a regularly scheduled Board meeting. I'm not sure when, but an announcement in the paper declared that a section of road not far from our place was to be surfaced with blacktop. This is big news – since the clear majority of our town roads have always been maintained in a crushed granite state. To some, the report is a sign of welcome progress. The boss couldn't be happier. I, on the other hand, found the thought downright depressing.

You see, to me, a part of the rural character of our township has always been gravel roads. The idea of living where the blacktop ends carries with it a certain amount of romance – heck, they even wrote a song about it. I like the feel of crushed gravel under my feet and the sound vehicles and their tires create as they rumble past our place.

"The dust and the noise, you can have it," the boss exclaims. "And the way they drive so fast past our house up to the corner, they can't pave it soon enough for me."

"Over my dead body," I retorted. "Our road will be the last one paved if I have anything to say in the matter."

47

"That might just work out fine," she giggled. "A speed bump right in front of our house – that will slow traffic down!"

*****

When we first took possession of our place in the country, we acquired a rural route number, a party-line telephone and a working outhouse. Years before cell phones and computers, our only connection to the outside world was controlled by the neighbor lady's gift of gab, a pair of rabbit ears on the TV and the postman.

Of the three, the roadside mailbox on a post continues steadfast – a true rural icon. Think about it. In 1737, Benjamin Franklin, referred to as the Father of the United States Postal System, was appointed postmaster of Philadelphia. For a fee of one penny, he delivered mail directly to the homes of Philadelphia citizens. By 1775, the Continental Congress appointed him postmaster general of North America. Over time, communication technology has grown leaps and bounds, yet the mailbox has remained relatively the same since 1858 when street letter boxes were first installed.

"Neither snow nor rain nor heat nor gloom of night stays these couriers from the swift completion of their appointed rounds," reads the adopted motto of the U.S. Postal Service. For nearly thirty years, our mailbox has stood tall and allowed their motto to ring true. Our letter box continues to link us to the outside printed world.

Blackberries, once only known for their contributions to pies and homemade wine, are now representative of the modern hand held communication world. In the blink of an eye, my friend from Washington D.C. can visit our home personal computer via his pocket-sized Blackberry unit.

Pods, only a short time ago, were reserved for peas and beans. Today, for the new generation, they communicate music libraries, photos, videos, games and calendars.

Satellites, once upon a time, served only to beam secrets from the sky to governments around the globe. Nowadays, dishes on every other rural home grab a hundred television channels out of thin air.

This past year, we broke down and purchased a satellite dish package to add to our own arsenal of personal computers, cell phones, telephones and the old standby – our mailbox. Hanging on the mailbox post is a newspaper tube, yet another daily source of information. That is the extent of our worldly communication possessions.

All things electronic are fine until the power fails, batteries die, or storms pass by – yet the mailbox endures – until someone runs it over. That was the case earlier this week.

"Did you hear that noise?" the boss questioned.

Out front, in the pre-dawn darkness, an inattentive driver had run the corner stop sign, skidded across our front lawn and driveway – barely missing the 100-year old locust tree, but did manage to take out the mailbox. When the sun rose I found our faithful letter box, crippled and in pieces, strewn across the lawn. I temporarily propped it up in hopes the mailman would honor his motto and deliver that day.

Later, the ill-fated driver apologized and offered to pay for a new post and box. By week's end, a new replacement should be installed. Perhaps, I'll upgrade and discover a new-fangled model that plugs in and glows in the dark.

DUBAY

The inscription reads, "Son of a Menominee Indian Princess, Son-in-Law of Chief Oshkosh – Treaty Maker, Interpreter, Indian Trader, Firm Friend of White Man." Those words grace a large, polished granite headstone of John Baptiste DuBay, who lived in the area from 1810 – 1887 and was buried in nearby Knowlton Cemetery. As the crow flies, that's just a few miles north of our place, on the opposite side of the Wisconsin River. A state historical marker in his honor also stands along our side of the river, near a cranberry bog and county campground, both named DuBay.

The sign talks about the remnants of this fur trader and frontiersman's trading post, that lie at the bottom of the lake also bearing his name – and according to locals, the flowage created by damming the Wisconsin River in 1942, also covered a cemetery near the post. The dam was primarily created to generate power for paper mills to the south and provide flood control in the spring. As a result, it backed up over 6,700 acres, created more than 42 miles of shoreline and takes in the flow of 12 inlet streams. There's plenty of open water for speed, sail and pontoon boaters, while its backwaters and islands are home to fishers and hunters.

Lake DuBay has become our summer home of sorts – since the boss and I long ago gave up the dream of a cabin "up north", trading that idea instead for a floating cottage on the sprawling body of water in our own backyard. It was on her birthday numbered forty that we took the plunge, so to speak. "Mom's Boat" was christened and ever since, evening and weekend pontoon outings on the lake have provided the necessary escape from our daily routine. Over the years, whether fishing, swimming, or just plain touring, we've learned to love all the huge lake offers.

Fishing opportunities abound, with nearly every native game fish species at hand – the exception being sturgeon and trout. But in the case of sturgeon, one need only to look downstream, just over the dam – as they're known to bump their snouts on the gates. Recently, white bass – of the Wolf River variety – have shown up in creels of fishermen seeking walleye and panfish. My good friend DNR Dale, and others in the know, aren't too keen on the idea of these recent invaders. You see, this unauthorized plant may cause havoc down the line, when competition for forage fish ensues.

As for our family, we spend most our fishing capital on smallmouth bass and walleye. Working the shoreline, docks and inlet creeks, hardly an outing goes by that doesn't reward us with a share of the bounty. According to local fishing guides, DuBay is an under-rated fishery and contains pike and musky, with trophy musky in the 45 to 50-inch range. Given current gas prices, local musky hunters may do well to stay close to home and give DuBay a try.

When fishing gets slow, we might head for a deluxe burger or fish fry at Saloon DuBay in Knowlton, or else enjoy a drink at the Tiki Bar at Antlers Bridge. More often, it's grilling brats on the pontoon, or watching the sail boat races or water ski shows at South Beach. Then there's always the simple pleasure of looking for driftwood on the shoreline. Oops! State officials have recently warned that removing driftwood is illegal, and violators could face fines. But, that's another story.

At the time the lake was fashioned with a dam and dike in 1942, the original headstone for its namesake was replaced by a beautiful piece of Wausau granite, thanks to George Mead Sr. of Consolidated Papers, Inc. I'm not sure why I drove past the gravesite for so many years with out stopping, but since the day it happened, my appreciation for the area's history has certainly been rekindled and the name DuBay has taken on new meaning.

THIS BENCH NOT FOR SALE

Something dear to my heart disappeared recently. Not a relative, friend, or pet – in fact, it was an inanimate object – a piece of family furniture – a gift from my kids. You see, someone came on our land and helped themselves to a bench, nestled on the edge of an opening in the woods – a spot reserved for banding spring woodcock. Trespass and theft – in one quick swoop.

It was not just a bench, it was a Leopold bench built by No. 2 son. A Father's Day present, one of several built for this aging father, who has discovered the joy of resting spots – strategically positioned around the back "40".

The bench was a simple piece of furniture – which by design was beautiful, both in its simplicity and in the eye of the beholder. A bench made from six boards and a handful of bolts and screws. Its value was not in material cost – instead, its worth was measured in family possession and what it represented.

After all, it was at a farm along the Wisconsin River downstream from here near Baraboo, that Wisconsin's most famous conservationist, Aldo Leopold, designed and made famous this style of bench – forever known as the Leopold bench. His family used wood retrieved from the river each spring to build benches, tables and assemble their weekend cabin retreat they called the "Shack". The bench, now found across the country, caught the eyes of his followers and remains a symbol of his being.

Our bench was of more modern design – using treated wood to withstand outdoor elements and screws and bolts in place of nails to increase its sturdiness. As benches go, it was well-made, having only one owner and low rear end mileage. But it was not for sale!

By my count, we have a total of six benches scattered over our property. One, our oldest, rests at the end of the field near a trail that leads to the creek. Besides being a convenient stop during the deer gun season, it will serve me well when No. 2 son and I build a wooden bridge over the creek crossing this summer.

Another is positioned upstream a hundred yards from the crossing, on a high bank overlooking a bend in the creek – a favorite spot for the boss and me to pause and ponder life's options together. It served the same purpose for good friend Mike and me last deer season.

A favorite is the one that can be seen from the kitchen window. It stands watch over the pond in the field and under the only "store bought" tree on our property, a golden Weeping Willow. Planted many years ago, as a sapling, it was our hope that in our waning years, it would throw ample shade and provide a shelter for a bench. The bench is in place, the willow is thriving and our aging process is right on schedule.

Two more benches are by the house, another back by the pond in the woods. The missing bench, who knows where?

That day we lost more than a piece of furniture. Vanished now is a slice of trust in our fellow man, as we were exposed to a certain element of society that feels no shame in taking other's property. But it was only a bench, simple in design and valued at only a few dollars. Here's hoping its new owner enjoys it as much as I did.

I doubt it.

FOR THE GOOD OF TICKS

Outdoor treks on warm summer days can be fraught with hazards. At times, travel through the woods and fields become downright miserable when one must compete with heat, mosquitoes, deer flies and ticks. Maybe it's just me, but this year it seems we have a bumper crop of ticks on the landscape. This past weekend alone, while putting out electric fence to keep the horses in, I brought home nearly thirty of these pesky, blood-sucking parasites – much to the boss's delight. During number one son's visit last month, he managed to locate almost a hundred ticks while filming the warbler migration in the river bottoms.

Waiting to affix themselves to warm-blooded hosts that pass on by, ticks lay in wait on knee-high grass and shrubs. Like mosquitoes, they can detect heat emitted or carbon dioxide respired, then hitch a ride as unsuspecting souls brush by their perches. Tales of flying or jumping ticks are false – and while their ability to drop off a perch may be true, I have yet to see them falling from trees. Once they climb aboard, harpoon-like digits, protruding out their mouths, allow the rascals to anchor themselves under our skin – making it difficult to remove the pests once they latch on. The digits are attached to the shaft of a tubular mandible, where blood extracted from the host flows. They suck until they're engorged – several times their normal size. If not plucked off, they will eventually fall to the ground, lay their eggs and die – and so goes the cycle – egg, larva, nymph and adult.

Some say temperature change and length of daylight effect and increase tick activity. If so, last week's heat and summer solstice could have marked a peak in tick goings-on, but keep in mind, they're really only dormant when snow covers the ground. The dogs and I find them late into fall while hunting grouse. In spring, the infamous day arrives, all too soon – most often, while turkey hunting is underway.

What purpose do ticks serve, anyhow? As far as that goes, what earthly good are mosquitoes, deer flies and spiders? Well, they're all spokes in the wheel of life, each providing for something else up and down the food chain. Mosquitoes feed swallows, frogs, toads and bats, who, by the way, eat literally thousands every night. Deer flies, my least favorite companion afield, are candy for dragonflies, swallows, flycatchers and kingbirds. But, my real heroes are the predators that control tick populations naturally – like several species of wasps, which lay their eggs into the bodies of ticks. After the eggs hatch, the larvae feed on the tick's internal tissues and then emerge, ultimately killing the host tick.

Gamebirds like turkey, pheasant and quail are known to consume mass quantities of ticks. Noisy cousin guinea hens and free ranging chickens are both quite fond of ticks and optimum tick control has been calculated at 1 bird per acre. Years ago, we kept a few pair of guineas and yes, they put our rooster chickens to shame in the noise department. By some accounts, wild turkeys are very effective predators of ticks across the country and can consume up to 200 a day, while pheasants can account for about 50 ticks daily. Our local flock of turkeys are "grazing" these days alongside the horses. Hopefully, ticks are on their menu. Other local tick predators include grackles, cowbirds, mice and ants.

Ants? Correlations between ant and tick densities have been studied for years, but unfortunately, no concluding evidence has surfaced that ant predation is a major factor in controlling tick numbers in our neck of the woods. However, in the south, fire ants are documented as effective tick killers. Recently, just out of curiosity, number two son and I conducted an experiment of our own. While passing by one of the numerous anthills out back, we dropped a tick on top of the heap. Within seconds – twelve, to be exact – an ant grabbed ahold of our "poor" subject and presently hauled him down into the recesses of the colony hill. We concluded that avoiding ticks is possible by spending time around anthills – but as number two quickly learned, ants bite and crawl up legs in a hurry.

Unfortunately, controlling tick populations and as far as that goes, most pests, is a never-ending battle – best left to natural means. While the thought of pest management by natural predation is appealing, in the long run, learning to live and play in their home may be our only option. However, cheering on our resident turkey flock, ant colonies and other "predators" won't hurt.

WORDS FROM LEOPOLD

A while back, I traveled downstream to the land of Leopold and a national workshop which was held at the newly constructed Aldo Leopold Legacy Center near Baraboo. Built on the site where this great man passed away in 1948 while fighting a grass fire on a neighbor's farm, it stands nestled in the woods near the land, the Wisconsin River and the famous "Shack" that inspired his masterpiece, *A Sand County Almanac*.

The Center houses the staff of the Aldo Leopold Foundation (ALF), which oversees priceless archives that pay testament to the man and his legacy. It is the primary depository of his writings, unpublished manuscripts, journals, correspondence, sketches, photographs, and tools he used on the land. The facility also maintains a photographic archive of over 1000 images from the 1930's and 40's of the Leopold family and friends.

It was a weekend of creative writing, teaching outdoors, natural history, reading the landscape, sustainability and quotes – lots of quotes. A master wordsmith, it is Leopold's words that endure – in the end, jumping off the paper and into the reader's head. Keynote speaker, Dr. Richard Jurin, University of Northern Colorado noted, "His genius was in his writing."

The following passage was written in the forward of the *Almanac* the year he died and a year before it was published. "Like winds and sunsets, wild things were taken for granted until progress began to do away with them. Now we face the question whether a still higher 'standard of living' is worth its cost in things natural, wild, and free. For us of the minority, the opportunity to see geese is more important than television, and the chance to find a pasque-flower is a right as inalienable as free speech."

His words and his books continue to inspire folks across the country and throughout the world. ALF reports that over two million copies have been printed and translated into nine languages. The Legacy Center now creates a place for individuals to feel and see first-hand the works of this man with such grand insight. His words, which rang true in 1948, still ring true today.

"There are two spiritual dangers in not owning a farm. One is the danger of supposing that breakfast comes from the grocery, and the other that heat comes from the furnace."

Dr. Jurin and other speakers at the workshop went to great lengths to bring the relevance of Leopold's words from the 1940s into today's terms. What held true back then, holds true now – perhaps more so. "Civilization has so cluttered this elemental man-earth relation with gadgets and middlemen that awareness of it (the land) is growing dim...All ethics so far evolved rest upon a single premise: that the individual is a member of a community of interdependent parts. His instincts prompt him to compete for his place in the community, but his ethics prompt him also to co-operate."

This environmental disconnect, or a nature deficit disorder – any way one puts it – has resulted in the general public's detachment from the land. It is perhaps, more than anything else, the single, leading problem we face as society struggles with a boat load of environmental issues.

There are examples galore, but one that hit close to home when number one son wrote home from school out east, "Bobolinks are way less common here (Rhode Island) than they are in our neighborhood, in fact there are only a few places in the state with breeding populations. I was excited to find a breeding pair right behind my apartment on the university-owned farm that I like to jog through. Well tonight, I was pretty bummed by what I found on my evening run (he attached a photo of an adult bobolink perched on a row of freshly mowed hay). I had not personally seen any fledglings, so I have to assume that they lost the nest that by now probably contained relatively large young. I hope I'm wrong."

No one group of people is closer to the land than farmers. With soil under their fingernails and an eye for the health of their land, even they, like the rest of us, show signs of disconnect with nature. Farmers, lawyers, teachers, bankers and especially today's youth could all do well by reading and appreciating the words of this great man – Aldo Leopold.

Then perhaps, something as simple and precious as a single nest of fledglings saved by a later mowing could be banked for future generations.

VACATION EAST

Footprints in the water – an idiom depicting circles of calm in an ocean of rolling waves and ripples. That's what naturalists call the tell-tale mark left by the giant whale as it thrust its tail, propelling the beast into a dive hundreds of feet below the surface. Once thought to be oil slicks left by the blubber-filled whales, the footprints drew a path for hunters to follow. The boss, number one son and I tracked a few ourselves a few years ago, a long way up the creek.

We had pointed our beaks east and ended up on a whale and puffin watch tour off the coast of Maine, during a visit with our son, who was attending graduate school. Twenty miles off the North Atlantic shore is where we spotted our first Northern Fin Whale. At sixty-feet long and weighing around 150,000 pounds, they are the second largest living animal, right behind the Blue Whale.

After leaving a footprint on the water's surface, it would dive up to 800 feet and feed on small schooling fish, krill, or squid – by opening its jaws and inhaling up to 18,000 gallons of water and twenty pounds of krill in a single gulp. Over the course of a three-hour feeding spree, one Fin Whale can consume 4,000 pounds of food a day – that's two tons!

For more than an hour, our solitary whale put on quite a performance and ended the show with a "logging" – a term I can certainly relate to – one used to describe a brief nap taken between

61

feedings. Our excursion – with air temperatures ranging from eighty degrees on shore to forty degrees out at sea – also led us to an island inhabited by a wide array of gulls, terns and alcids. My binoculars, camera and pencil were busy as I observed and recorded many new birds to my "life list". Besides the Common Puffin, we saw Razorbills, Red Phalaropes, Greater Shearwaters, Gannets, Fulmars, Wilson's Petrels and Artic Terns. Several of these were far from shore feeding, while other were still tending nests on isolated island refuges.

Of the eight new observations, our favorite by far were the puffins, who along with the razorbills of the Alcids group, come ashore only to breed in large colonies. They swim underwater using their wings, winter at sea and sport red, blue-grey and ivory parrot-like bills.

Ashore, we traveled to nearby Acadia National Park, a 35,000-acre federal recreational area containing miles of scenic seacoast and spectacular rock formations – as well as islands, forests, lakes and mountains. With over 120 miles of hiking trails and a never-ending series of well-maintained roads throughout the park, we saw it all.

Number one son explored the rocky shoreline, fishing and taking pictures along the way. We all ascended to the top of Cadillac Mountain, reached the summit and watched the sun set with a large group of tourists. At 1,532 feet in elevation, the peak is the highest point along the North Atlantic seaboard and is the first place to view sunrise in the United States during the fall and winter months. Fortunately for these old legs, a road ended just below the summit's crest.

A bit more solitude would have suited us better, but it was very refreshing to see so many folks in such a beautiful spot enjoying nature – each in their own way. With that many acres, it was easy to get "lost". We ate lunch at a bar and grill over the water at Bar Harbor, where salmon, shrimp and lobster were on our menu – and later in the day, a trip to Maine's famous LL Bean outdoor goods store was in order.

When we returned to Wisconsin, we were greeted by the season's first crickets and a chance to experiment with their temperature predicting talents. Dolbear's Law, formulated around 1896, tells us to count the number of chirps in 14 seconds, then add 40 to get the current outdoor temperature.

I sat on the back porch and counted. Twenty-eight chirps in 14 seconds. Adding forty gave me 68 degrees. My brand-new LL Bean outdoor brass thermometer read exactly 68 degrees outside the kitchen window. Imagine that!

SUMMER'S SHADES OF GREEN

A balloonist floating over the Wisconsin River valley had a bird's eye view of the landscape. "You don't realize how many different shades of green exist until you look from above," he remarked. "Wisconsin is really green."

Shades of summer green – grasses, trees, bushes, ferns, weeds and crops – as far as the eye can see are with us now. Green leaves of all the plants are acting as solar collectors, their cells gathering power from the sun. Photosynthesis at work, turning sunlight into sugar – using water and releasing oxygen and in the process creating the green pigment chlorophyll. To follow-up the aviator's observation, I paused out back the other night and gazed over the tree line surrounding our field of prairie grass.

The family weeping willow stands out in a world of green – its leaves with whitish undersides in concert with bright green topsides, paint an image of sage brush silver-green. Waxy aspen leaves tremble, reflecting yellow-green, while green maple leaves appear dipped in shades of red and purple. Dull green birch leaves cling to drooping branches and sway in the wind. The oaks at the end of the field are much bolder; their shiny dark green leaves are accompanied by splashes of young yellow-green acorns.

The prairie grasses of our field, supported by green stems and leaves now flaunt colored flowers. Leadplant, milkweed, indigo, blazing star and lupine – just to name a few, turn a mundane green field ablaze.

64

Across the road is a field of corn, waist high and sprouting several layers of green leaves, pale yellow silk topped ears and stalks that point to the clouds. Young, succulent soybeans down the road are taking on a deeper green hue and attract grazing deer at dawn and dusk, while freshly cut hayfields in every direction, littered with thousand-pound round bales, serve as dinner tables for families of cranes.

The swamps and bogs north and west of here are also green with summer growth of cattails, alder, sedges, bulrushes and lilies. Bogs, like those bordering nearby cranberry operations are dominated by sphagnum mosses, sedges, leatherleaf and laurel.

Our backyard lawn, complete with assorted weeds and seedlings, battles the mower and grows green despite a lack of rain and fertilizer.

In a few months, when days become shorter, chlorophyll production will slow down and uncover other, more vibrant pigments. And with that, grasses, ferns, shrubs and trees will turn the colors of fall.

Until then, enjoy summer's shades of green!

DAKOTA

A hoot owl called out three times behind the house that fateful Friday night – perhaps announcing to the river valley that my beloved bird dog and best pal had passed away.

The phone rang earlier that day at my in-law's house after a morning of cutting firewood. I left lunch abruptly and speechless, weak in the knees and choking back tears – Dakota was dead.

I've buried many dogs along the creek over the past thirty years, but this one hit me like a bolt of lightning. I was not ready for his untimely death and still am not sure what happened. No warnings of any kind, no indications of trouble brewing – heck, except for the fact that he was pushing eleven years old and was a few pounds overweight, Dakota was the picture of health. Hadn't he put his paws on my chest as I sat by my desk that very morning? And ate some food and drank some water? Apparently, his heart just stopped beating and he died peacefully in his sleep.

With a heart of gold and fire in his eyes, Dakota was more than just a bird dog. He was my friend and constant companion for more than a decade. Early in his career, he earned a blue ribbon and trophy at a wild bird field trial. We traveled a half dozen times to the western prairies of the Dakotas and eastern Montana, where he learned to savor the aroma of pheasant, sharptail grouse and Hungarian partridge. But it was ruffed grouse and woodcock from his home state that he longed for year in and year out.

Rocky, Dakota's younger brother and best buddy for eight

years, now sits by my side – then puts his paws on my chest as I sit by the desk – like his brother before him did a thousand times. He looks deep into my eyes and seems to ask, "Why?" I find myself at a loss for words and tears once again run down my cheeks.

Dakota's picture hangs on the office wall while his death hangs heavy on my heart. Eventually, the hurt will subside as fond recollections of his life take over. Having occupied a special position in my soul, the emptiness will fill slowly with his lasting memories.

Many years ago, I heard a hoot owl call out three times behind the house on a frigid Thanksgiving Day. Dakota's great-great-grandfather Buck had passed away peacefully in his sleep that afternoon as I sat perched in a deer stand. They are now both buried down by the creek. No. 2 son picked out a special spot near the weeping willow tree alongside the pond for Dakota and covered the grave with select boulders from a rock fence near the house. With a bench under the tree, one day soon I will sit for a spell and say goodbye.

After all, as the saying goes, time heals all wounds.

DEATH'S DOOR ESTUARY

It's an annual pilgrimage that takes us from our place along the creek to a special retreat near Door County's Death's Door. Around the corner from the infamous passage between Washington Island and tip of the peninsula lies the Mink River Estuary and a cabin we call home for a couple of days each year.

One of the most pristine freshwater estuaries in the country, its spring-fed wetlands creates a river that mixes with Lake Michigan at Rowley's Bay. The estuary is an important fish spawning and bird migration area and many rare and uncommon birds can be observed. On this trip we saw more in the common variety of gulls, herons, swans, mergansers, cormorants and a few unusual pelicans. But in the end it was the gulls and terns that stole the show during our visit.

From dawn to dusk, hundreds of gulls and terns hunted and scavenged by crisscrossing the bay, swooping and diving while making a living snatching hapless minnows swimming close to the surface. The stars of the show were the terns – plummeting from thirty feet high, hitting the water with a smack, going completely underwater and with luck, flying off carrying prize fish in their beaks.

Squawking and crying out non-stop, many of the larger gulls pensively stood watch over their domain, high atop the peak of the three-story lodge across the road from our bayside cabin. They would take turns flying off to forage and while floating on the water like ducks, they would hang around diving cormorants and mergansers, hoping to grab leftovers. Then back to sentry duty on the red roof top, marked with white chalk-like gull poop. We spotted several pelicans on the bay and they too would follow the small groups of diving fish eaters, snatching what they could.

A few years ago, in another location, I watched a tribe of seventy pelicans fishing a small mill pond. Side by side, they paddled through lily pad infested shallows and drove luckless bullheads to one another. It was synchronized scooping of the shallows and when one would catch a fish, it would peel out of line and swallow their meal head first, and then move back in formation.

Our window to the avian world of an estuary this year revealed a community working together to survive. It was a scene in constant motion, never silent – a picture worthy of canvas or a few words in print. Hunters and scavengers, grabbing prey or leftovers, putting forth a spectacular show on a stage unique to a location only a couple hours' drive from our place along the creek.

Wisconsin harbors hundreds of similar gems in all directions. Who needs the Grand Canyon when other wonders of the world are right in our own backyard?

A DOVE SURVEY

What is it about an early spring morning that exhilarates us so? Perhaps it is the new dawn that washes away layers of time from yesterday, or the fresh air that clears ones head without much thought. For me, it is being among the creatures that stir as the sun slowly rises in the east.

That is the way it was on a past bluebird day when rising before dawn and traveling south for an hour with my mother, June, now approaching her 90th year. Together, we participate in an annual national mourning dove call-count survey for the US Fish and Wildlife Service. Our route, number 0910, begins just north of Wautoma and extends to just shy of Princeton in Green Lake and Waushara counties. 20 miles in length, it contains 20 stops, or listening stations at 1-mile intervals.

Since 1983, we have conducted the same two-hour survey exactly one half hour before sunrise – 4:51 am until 6:48 am – and precisely 3 minutes for counting at each stop while driving 35 miles per hour between pauses. We recorded the number of doves heard calling while stopped and the number of doves seen while driving and stopped.

This particular spring, we documented a total of 47 doves heard and 20 seen. That compares very close to that of the previous year's count and lies in company with the top ten years since we began in 1983. Those results and those of past years were submitted to the Division of Migratory Bird Management in

Laurel, Maryland. There they will compile the results from across the nation.

There were cranes and lupines, turkeys and hickories, deer and aspen, pheasant and willow, herons and cattails, rails and sedges, blackbirds and oak, vultures and hillsides, wood ducks and alder, warblers and hazelnuts, geese and cornfields, teal and lily pads, squirrels and acorns, muskrats and pine cones.

We also heard more than the mournful cooing of doves. In the background, was the gobble of male turkeys, the crowing of male pheasants, the ever-present bugling of cranes, the hooting of owls, gulping of bitterns, gurgling of warblers, honking of geese and raucous robins.

And a magnificent sunrise at stop number 6, always the same numbered stop, at precisely 5:21 am we greet the sun. With a light cloud bank, a red sky painted the eastern horizon and once again, took our breath away. By stop number 8, it disappeared, making way to blue skies and warming temperatures.

With stop 20 in sight we reflected on the day and past 600 miles and 30 years' worth of surveys. We rounded the bend and were rewarded with three doves on the shoulder of the road. As we stopped, we nodded in agreement – once again, it has been worth the effort.

CRICKETS AND OTHER SIGNS OF AUTUMN

It happens every August. A cutting expectation sets in – sometimes early in the month, more often towards the end. Exactly what triggers this disorder remains a mystery, despite several theories by experts. For those of us afflicted with this ailment, it's specific to the host and has only one cure.

For this scribe, the anticipation starts with the stridulating of crickets out our back door. Their chirping, produced by rubbing forewing "teeth" together, calls out to others of their kind and in the process, activates something lying deep within me – an anticipation – a yearning for yet another fall season.

The short-term weather forecast calls for a small pardon from the lengthy summer heat wave. Long-term calls for more heat, yet tell-tale signals of fall are popping up all over the landscape. Slowly, but surely the seasons change.

On my way to town and work this week, I couldn't help but see signs of autumn coming to pass. While getting into my truck, an assembly of blackbirds and grackles – several families worth – flocked together and made a racket that filled the treetops behind the house. Their gabble signaled a turning point – from the backyard to the cattail marshes they march – stepping stones towards fall migration.

A longing hunter – by wishing so hard – can see what others pass by without notice. While driving down the road, I spot browning ferns, yellow and red poison ivy leaves and scarlet lowland maples. Box elder and popple add to the mix and begin to pale against the deep greens of summer.

Fueling the fire are molting sandhill cranes, potato harvesters at work, fall hunting catalogs and sporting goods sale flyers in the mailbox. Gaggles of urban Canada geese tease me each morning as they graze on mowed lawns. Any one of these signals, or all of them put together, activate a launch sequence of events that lead to my favorite time of the year.

Like a chameleon, or snake, my skin sheds its appearance by the season and my surroundings. I become a hunter and join thousands of my kind in the fields and woods. We're drawn by a force beyond our control – a power outside our command.

The role of hunting in human evolution has demonstrated to researchers that early hunter-gathering men demonstrated an altered state of testosterone, while the endorphin and adrenaline rush experienced by modern hunters has also been well-documented. Upland, waterfowl and deer hunters have been "wired" for science and produce heartbeats over 120 beats a minute during hunting situations. Beyond all that, the physiological excitement that attracts one to hunt also produces a sense of well-being and is strengthened by anticipation, preparation and post-hunt activities.

The cure? The only known one involves participation. If you are not prone to this burden, chances are you know someone who is. For those of you that live with the afflicted, you struggle to understand why. A dear neighbor lady once told me, "I don't know what happens to my son – he's a different person come deer season. Just the thought of the approaching season makes him crazy."

The boss of our house, a non-hunter, has learned to deal with our family's obsession with the fall hunting season. You see, after several decades of living with men who suffer from the misery, she seems to have come to terms with the annual event. She savors the peace and quiet it affords her while we're off in the woods.

Can you feel and see it coming? Look hard, the signs are all around.

THE HOMECOMING

It was a homecoming of sorts, when No.1 son returned recently for a short, two-week visit. Back from the university and mountains of Nevada, his plans included – much to my delight – a day devoted to his old man.

He and I traveled upstream to a place we'd both been before, a location dear to him, as well as his brother, several close friends and yours truly. A river that flows through our minds and beckons year after year, especially when the leaves turn shades of fall. A river that runs through county, state and federal lands and offers those of us that follow a bounty of fish and fowl.

This outing we were after smallmouth bass with fly and spinning rods on a river that cascades leisurely among a thousand boulders before tumbling swiftly over a falls – all the time singing the song of water in motion. We fished above and below the waterfalls and for a while I sat on the high banks and watched as my son handled his fly rod with the skill of a master. He can fling a streamer with precision – from one boulder eddy to the next. When something like a large rock gets in the river's way, the water is forced to slow down, change direction and whirlpool. He knows fish like that – laying in wait for food to swing by. I watched as he stood high on top of a car sized boulder – my son, no longer boy, but a man of talent, handling life as skillfully as he handles a fly rod.

As I get older, finding pleasure in undemanding tasks becomes easier, like watching from afar as my son fished in quiet solitude.

75

I felt warm all over, keeping watch as he waded the rocky river, fly rod in hand and camera around his neck. Sitting safely on my perch in the riverbank pines, I found myself envying his strong, young legs, as he deftly maneuvered the boulders.

The sun glistened against the rippling water and I drifted off in reflection. The sky above was blue, the wind gentle and the woods was choked in green and smelled of pine and popple. I paused to write, then looked up and saw he'd caught another bass.

The only sound I heard was from the wind and the river – their songs competing, as a current of air slipped through the pines and water rolled around the boulders. I wrote down some thoughts and then looked up again to see my son moving upstream, only to stop and cast once more. Sitting in the shade among the waist high bracken ferns, I pondered a question friend Brian once posed: what makes the sound? Was it the wind, or the pine branches holding the needles? Was it the rushing water, or the boulders? Without the boulders, our river would cease to sing. Absent the flowing river, the boulders would lay silent. I stop pondering just long enough to look up again at my son. I whistled and he waved while changing flies.

Together, the wind and needles strike up a conversation with my imagination. A babbling river brings tales from far upstream to my mind's eye. Together, wind, needles, water and boulders sing songs of inspiration.

Again, my son stepped into a stretch of open stream, glanced my way and took a picture.

It was a homecoming of sorts – short, sweet and over in a blink. But in between his arrival and departure, No. 1 son managed to squeeze in two family get-togethers, a wedding, separate musky and trout fishing trips up north and a very special day with his old man on a river we both know so well.

Autumn

"Everyone needs a secret spot, or two – covert places we call our own – I have a couple. No doubt, so do you."

SEPTEMBER WINDS

I long for September all year round. It marks the beginning of a hunter's new season. Given the authority, I would declare September 1st New Year's Day.

The hunt begins in less than a week. Goose and dove hunters will go afield first, followed later in the month by those pursuing bear, grouse, turkey, deer, woodcock and waterfowl. It is a busy month indeed for those that call outdoors home in the fall. Add late season musky hunting to the list and spare time on the September calendar for sportsmen disappears.

Overnight, the transition from summer to fall will take place. A predicted cold front – with temperatures at night in the 40s and daytime highs in the 50s – will remind us that fall is at our doorsteps. While it is still a month before the brilliant colors of October surround us, something deep inside hunters and migrant birds is stirring now. Following gun dogs, or sitting in secluded blinds, hunters will enjoy front row seats in nature's migratory theater and the transformation of seasons.

Last week, while sitting around our fire pit, we witnessed the first wave of nighthawks as they began their gentle movements south. Travel to South America takes a long time and fueling the voyage involves lots of insects – available in the sky as they pass on through our river valley. Monarch butterflies have also begun their southward journey – gone by the first frost and by October's end, basking in Mexican sunshine. By the tail end of

September, blue-winged teal and wood ducks will be packing their bags.

Like many of our neighbors, we have tempted local and migrant critters to a food plot. Strategically located at the end of our prairie field and in range of the kitchen table spotting scope, ours has offered endless hours of entertainment – especially in the fall. Recently, several turkeys have been stars of the daily show and visit our plot more than once a day. While there, they make the most of what it has to offer. The buckwheat, sorghum and clover were planted rather late, yet have responded to ample rainfall and now provide cover and food for a wide variety of wildlife. In the case of our turkeys, the buckwheat is flowering and attracting insects – a protein laden food source for birds of all stripes.

Deer are working over the neighbor's soybean fields and several mature bucks have been seen grazing at dusk. Their antlers will soon shed their reddish-brown velvet coatings and shine bright as archers wait along their runways between bedding and feeding areas.

By mid-month, hunters and their bird dogs will work the uplands for grouse and woodcock and the sound of bells may be heard as they comb alder and popple stands. The baying of hound dogs will fill the northwoods as the bear hunt will be in full swing. And by the end of the month, waterfowlers will roam marshes, rivers and lakes for ducks and geese.

Let the hunt begin.

*****

In a technical sense, autumn's equinox arrives in late September when the Sun crosses the equator and the duration of day and night stands equal.

82

But fall blows in with a vengeance when cold fronts and blustery winds sweep down from Canada. When average temperatures drop more than twenty degrees and suddenly autumn unfolds before our very eyes. October is right around the corner and now's the time to taste the sounds, sights and smells of the season.

Northern geese have begun to pass through in noisy gaggles. Cranes trumpet from nearby harvested fields and secluded marshes. Wood ducks cry as they patrol backwater sloughs and river bottoms. On rare occasions, male ruffed grouse drum, rooster pheasants crow and tom turkeys gobble. Buck deer will soon grunt for mates and from hedgerow thickets migrating songbirds will warble. Autumn music is with us until the season's final curtain call.

The brilliant shades of yellow, orange, and red overrule the green pigments in leaves that thrive only in warm weather. As temperatures drop and daylight hours diminish, autumn pigments kick in and leaves transform like magic, sometimes overnight. Now is the moment to explore the countryside to view its full glory. Time is of essence as the winds of the season will eventually send the foliage to the forest floor.

For hunters, that means following the course of migrant game birds. For birders, it's time to keep an eye on the sky and in the bush. Throngs of juncos, warblers, fox sparrows and robins will invade central Wisconsin soon. Waterfowl and cranes are staging in large numbers throughout the state. Geese chase their flyways and woodcock slip in quietly – without fanfare and in the dark of night – their initial rides on the wave of northwesterly winds. Dogwood thickets and alder bottoms become transitory homes for woodcock – their secluded whereabouts only uncovered by investigating bird dogs and hunters.

Step outside, take a deep breath and smell the season. Fallen leaves, pine needles and brown grasses soaked in morning dew arouse our senses like nothing else. Exhale and see your breath for perhaps the first time since last winter. Enjoy the tang of frosty mornings and crisp moonlit nights. Until next spring, you'll smell nothing more refreshing.

October will light the first fire of the season in the woodstove – another milestone of the year. Outside our back door is a growing pile of oak firewood, thanks to brother-in-law Mike and father-in-law John – as well as assorted elm, maple and popple – thanks to the woods that envelops our creek. Together, in September, we greet the chill that accompanies the season.

OCTOBER ODYSSEY

It's a recurrent dream. One I hope comes to pass this fall. A journey without boundaries – an odyssey of sorts – to places I have yet to explore and several locations I know well. An autumn road trip, several weeks in length – just me and my bird dogs. Along the way, a rendezvous with good friends up north, a date with my sons on the Dakota prairies and maybe a new adventure that crosses the Missouri River.

It will be a slow voyage across the top of four states. Sleeping where I end up at night, hunting where opportunity knocks and pausing more often than necessary to let the dogs stretch. Hunting grouse and woodcock on the barrens and forests of northern Wisconsin – then ducks, pheasants and sharptails amidst the prairie potholes – all the while, seldom straying far from Highway 2 – perhaps all the way to Montana.

When the time is right, I'll meet up with No. 1 son on his way home from the mountains of Nevada. Together, we'll pick up No. 2 son in Bismarck, or Minot, or Fargo – wherever the plane drops him off. Before it gets dark, several ducks and pheasants will be added to a stew and washed down with strong prairie coffee.

Like many of you, time for me is measured by the intervals between Octobers. So, wake me when September arrives, because now it is summer and I am taking a nap – albeit, while I snooze, weekends will be occupied with lazy days floating and fishing on the river, attending weddings, celebrating birthdays, graduations and picnicking around the campfire ring. Evenings will slip away with homestead duties – cutting grass, gardening and home improvements. The boss and I will take a couple of overnight trips to gaze at waterfalls, lighthouses, wineries and other points of interest. Friends already gathered at our place this past weekend for a Father's Day summer bird dog training camp tradition.

During the long summer weeks, I will focus on work, earn more vacation leave and drift off from time to time – daydreaming of frost and falling leaves and a trip that will test my mettle. An idea whose time has come and is knocking on my door. Maybe, just maybe, if I begin packing now, it will arrive faster.

It may be a dream, but it's a vision I have – a journey to ponder. If it comes to pass, it will be a dream come true – an October odyssey. Do me a favor, wake me when September arrives.

What are you dreaming about?

*****

This report came from way down the creek. From the land of race horses, bourbon and baseball bats. Since the late 1800s, home of the Kentucky Derby, handcrafted ash and maple Louisville Sluggers and world renown distilled spirits aged in barrels.

You see, my real job – the one that pays the bills – had me in Kentucky, at a water resource conference on the banks of the Ohio River. My story began while driving south along an Indiana interstate. A cell phone call from No. 1 son on a mountaintop broke the monotony as he reported of a successful sage grouse hunt with his birddog Sue. He shared a story of also spotting a small herd of elk while friends with rifles and tags were over the hill in the next valley.

Later, while the conference was underway and I sat in one of several seminars, my mind wandered to a place along our creek waiting for friend, Pastor Craig to arrive. My thoughts drifted towards the weekend, when he, No. 2 son and I would pack the dogs and gear in trucks and head north – to a county that touches Lake Superior and is home to grouse, woodcock, bears and wolves. We would spend the better part of a week exploring its borders and hunting upland birds.

While the Under Secretary of Agriculture for Rural Development addressed the convention of more than a thousand water professionals, I confess to concentrating on my October odyssey beginning later that week. When he praised our combined leadership roles in providing safe drinking water to rural America, I plead guilty to wondering if I had enough shotgun shells and gear for the trip. And during a standing ovation for yet another dignitary, I admit to dreaming of bird dogs, tag alder and aspen stands.

While walking acres of booths in an exhibit hall extravaganza devoted to products and services available to the water industry, I contemplated the last time I oiled my hunting boots back home. That mindset disappeared when my cell phone rang twice in the hall – No. 1 son called again to report they had shot an elk and were packing it out of a mountainous wilderness area. Then, No. 2 son called and reported equally exciting news – he had just completed all the required tests for his pilot license.

That week I may have sipped Woodford Reserve bourbon, caressed a freshly handcrafted Louisville bat made of ash and admired a thoroughbred horse or two, but I'm here to say my thoughts were of our creek and the land of cheese, beer and the great northwoods.

By the time the ink dried on this story, I was on the road, my mind and compass both pointing north – closer to home and a hunting vacation.

RUFFED GROUSE CYCLES

Driving northbound last weekend on a two-lane highway, we were greeted by a contrasting light dusting of snow on open ground and still brilliant fall colors in the woods. We arrived Saturday afternoon at grouse camp, north of the tension zone and just shy of the south shores of Lake "Gitche Gumee".

For the better part of a week, a cabin on an inland lake became home as Pastor Craig, No. 2 son and I pursued the king of upland game birds, the ruffed grouse – and his migrating cousin, the American woodcock – who both share northwood habitats of aspen, alder and hardwood.

I met my first ruffed grouse as a teenager in the late 1960s. It exploded from a stand of scrub oak in Waushara County and sailed off unscathed. I stood mouth open, holding an empty shotgun shell and wondering what had just happened. It was my first ruffed grouse hunt during a "high" in their 10-year population cycle and now, forty years later, I found myself enjoying yet another high.

Ruffed grouse populations rise and fall on a ten-year cycle, and wildlife biologists agree, "In the Lake States, periods of abundance usually coincide with years ending in 0, 1 or 2, and the bottom of the depression in years ending with 5 or 6." From my personal observations, during depressed years, flush rates of 1 bird per hour are the norm. During a high that will rise to 5, or more per hour.

Day one of this year's hunt – after travel time to camp – afforded just enough time to get in a short, late afternoon foray to get things started. In less than an hour, our bird dogs found two grouse, five woodcock and one very annoyed porcupine. Rocky, No. 2 son's eight-year-old German shorthaired pointer pointed the rodent at the end of the day under a tipped over hemlock. Luckily for all involved, Rocky backed off and chose another path back to the truck.

Day two was much more productive. We managed to see 28 grouse and 27 woodcock and in the process – put enough birds in the fridge for good meal. The day began with a late migrant loon yodeling on our lake and ended when Rocky emerged from the woods carrying a plump grouse we thought had gotten away. The value of a well-trained bird dog comes into play more than once each season and this time was no exception.

Day three broke cold and frosty. Before entering the woods, snow began to fall in earnest and proceeded to paint evergreens and yellow, orange and red leaves white. Snow in October is not unusual, especially near Lake Superior. And while it may have dampened our hunting clothes, it didn't our spirits. Our flush rate declined a bit, but after three days and my column's deadline, we averaged 5 grouse per hour hunted.

For an upland bird hunter and their dogs, there is nothing like a ruffed grouse high.

SECRET SPOTS

Everyone needs a secret spot, or two. I have a couple. No doubt, so do you.

Covert places outdoors that we can call our own – filling needs within our souls. I visit one several times each fall, while following my bird dog deep into the woods northwest of our place. Suffice it to say, I can not reveal the location – just know it is located somewhere between here and there.

The path we follow, the dog and I, leads to a place dubbed the "church of whispering pines". By any standard, the plantation is small and surrounded by younger lowland aspen and alder, that for years stood tall above all else – ripe to catch the wind and speak softly to weary hunters and their dogs. The reference to the church undoubtedly came from the guilt cast from being pineward and hunting on Sunday mornings.

An hour's walk from the truck, it is a delightful place to stop and rest. A rusted trailer, long ago abandoned by loggers, sleeps besides the trail – providing a spot to lean a gun, relax tired feet and ponder. When the boys were young and toting BB guns, it doubled as a perch for aluminum can targets.

Over the span of nearly three decades and five generations of dogs, I have hiked back to the "church", which is far enough in to escape all man-made sounds – except for an occasional gunshot, far off in the distance. The dog, "Little Buck", follows in the tracks of his ancestors, nose to the ground, searching for the scent of partridge that drifts at the mercy of the wind along the forest floor. Standing the test of time, partridge scent is what brings us to this spot each fall.

For nearly twenty years, a close friend and hunting buddy, Craig, has shared this spot with me. I have never met another hunter with his drive and success and when it comes to grouse hunting – his accomplishments are that of local legend. His real secret spot is a camp up north that is about as far off the beaten path as you can go before you're on your way back out. It stands empty now – hunting at his grouse camp is on hold until further notice. You see, Craig got his marching orders from above and is spending time in a southern seminary. In his spare moments, he still goes afield – albeit in a much different setting, but with no less passion.

In a recent message, Craig noted, "The other morning, while dove hunting, I was thinking of all the great opening day trips we had together...The only thing missing was the sound of the bear hounds...I told the Bible Study group that I am teaching, about that great event, but they really didn't seem to care. I guess unless you haven't had the great pleasure of enjoying a moment like that, you just don't know what you are missing...I am really starting to miss the sound, smell, taste, and friendship of grouse and woodcock hunting...Only a couple more years, God willing, and we will be able to enjoy a few more trips together...Blessings, Craig"

There are special places we have all visited in the past and secret spots that await us in the future. Here's hoping you take pleasure in yours as much as I do mine.

STOP THE CLOCK

Last week, this week and perhaps the next are what my cousin from Sweden would call "stop the clock" moments. If only the full spectrum of fall's colors and weather could last for months, not just a few short-lived weeks. A yearly calendar containing twelve months of Octobers, would truly be a dream come true.

Who among us can gaze across the landscape at this moment in time without wonder? What power – beyond the science of it all – creates the brilliant shades of yellow, orange, and red? We know the green pigment in leaves is chlorophyll and thrives only in warm weather. As temperatures drop and daylight hours diminish, carotene and anthocyanin pigments persist and cause leaves to appear yellow and red respectively. Picture postcard beauty beyond description, lies in view and can soften even the hardest of souls. I dare to ponder – who really controls the paintbrush?

Time is of the essence for those of us that wait patiently for this time of the year.

For hunters, that means following the course of migrant game birds. For birders, it's time to keep an eye on the sky and in the bush. Throngs of juncos, fox sparrows and robins have invaded central Wisconsin. Cranes are staging. Geese are passing through in noisy gaggles and woodcock have slipped in quietly – without fanfare and in the dark of night – riding the wave of this week's northerly winds. Dogwood thickets and alder bottoms become their transitory homes – their secluded whereabouts only uncovered by investigating bird dogs and hunters.

Last week, good friend and hunting partner Mike, flew in from out west and shared his little piece of heaven on earth with the dogs and me. We watched as young aspen on his property turned from dull green to brilliant yellow in two days. Together with friends Dale and Jim, we followed the dogs during the day and found woodcock and grouse. Later in the evening, we sipped beer on the back porch, fussed with a puppy and shared a bag full of memories.

At dusk, we watched the woodcock fly to their evening roosts.

Some claim that woodcock migrate by the stars and the moon. Their internal compass allows the wandering bird to zero in to familiar wintering grounds near the gulf shores of Georgia, Alabama and Louisiana. Like robins, it is ultimately the cold weather, frost and freezing temperatures that limit their worm supplies. Together, they seek warmer climates and move south each fall in mass.

This week, frost has knocked on our door and leaves will drop in earnest. By week's end, the Hunter's Moon will appear. As it passes by, it becomes the largest, brightest and closest to the Earth as any other full moon of the year. With cloud cover lacking, it will illuminate the darkness. And with winds from the north, migrating woodcock will pass through with ease.

Go ahead, set your alarm and take a peek, just before midnight.

THE RUTTING SEASON

The rut is on.

The same circumstances that cause temperatures and leaves to drop, daylight hours to shorten and birds to migrate – send female whitetail deer into estrous and male bucks into their annual mating frenzy.

Along the roadways, motorists beware!

Along the creek bottom, a buck or two began leaving their calling cards last week. Oval scrapes on a nearby mowed trail – carved in the fallen leaves down to bare soil – mark their territories and let the girls and rival boys know who they are and where they have been. Left behind are hoof prints, body scent and overhead "lick" branches. A series of scrapes, fifty-yards apart, together with antler rubs on nearby trees, delineate male whitetail deer travel routes as they pass through our property. Research by others reveals that dominant, mature bucks extend their home range to around 5 square miles during the peak of the rut.

These three expressions of the season – scrapes, rubs and "lick' branches – will occupy the world of whitetails for a month, or more, with the first full week of November considered by many as the peak. Many devoted bowhunters schedule vacation time around the rut. Auto repair shops also prepare for their busiest time of the year.

Antler rubs begin to show up in October. Bucks pick trees and shrubs that suit their fancy. Yearling bucks tend to choose small diameter trees that have a lot of "give" to polish their antlers.

94

Larger, mature bucks select bigger diameter trees with less resistance. Monarchs of the forest prefer more sturdy adversaries – sometimes oak, or better yet, spruce, or alder in the lowlands.

Twigs hanging over scrapes invariably become "licking" branches – suspended limbs about five feet above the ground. The tip of the branch they have recently nibbled off, rubbed and licked, holds scent from glands around their eyes and oily forehead for receptive does.

Females pass by and after close inspection, judge their suitors by scrapes, rubs and "lick' branches. When the time is right, they hang around the area and await their return. With a home range of less than a square mile, does are never too far off.

Neighbor Ed stopped by with a fine, mature ten-point buck he tagged while bowhunting this past weekend. Following a bunch of does proved to be the buck's ultimate downfall. As I admired his polished antlers, I couldn't help but notice sticky pine pitch at their base. Several rows of young red pine along our property line have served as rubs for years. Sure enough, later inspection showed freshly stripped bark and running pine pitch.

Had his buck visited our 40 acres? Perhaps, but as luck would have it, No. 2 son spotted another ten-pointer out back on Monday – not too far from his gun deer stand.

If the mild weather holds out, this year's deer firearm season may very well overlap the rut. And until the older bucks wise up and realize their world has been invaded by the blaze orange army, the early hours of the hunt may be interesting indeed.

*****

When I was a young lad, the eve of the annual deer hunt was cause for sleepless nights and stomach aches. Like the night before Christmas, expectations ran high and dreams swirled in my head. I literally trembled in anticipation until the alarm clock rang opening morning.

My first season was in 1969 and father and I hunted the Nicolet National Forest near Langlade. Self-taught nimrods, we managed to stay out of the way of more experienced hunters and enjoyed ourselves immensely. I was driven by the desire to become a hunter, dad's participation was a labor of love – the love for his only son.

That first year, we joined a half million gun hunters, whose expectations were low and killed just 98,000 animals statewide. Hunter success matched expectations in the national forest, where deer populations were estimated at six per square mile in the fall. It took five seasons before I killed my first buck.

Forty seasons have come and gone. Wildlife officials warn hunters to expect shooting fewer deer this year than last – a campaign to keep hunter expectations low as the herd adjusts to heavy harvests over the past ten years, which amounts to nearly 5 million gun and bow kills.

Low expectations? I need only to think back forty years, when simply seeing a deer while hunting was noteworthy of discussion back at the café. Today's hunter recalls a few years ago, when we were told to harvest does like there was no tomorrow. Apparently, we have succeeded – the evidence that less deer grace the landscape is all around us.

Insurance companies announced another reduction in car-deer crashes in 2008. State department of transportation officials report, "The number of reported deer crashes per 100 million vehicle miles traveled peaked in 1994. In 1996, the rate declined sharply, tapering off through 2003, with a further decline to an average of 30 crashes per 100 million vehicle miles traveled in 2006 and 2007. There was a further decline in 2008."

A more dramatic sign can be seen in the woods. For the first time in memory, while grouse hunting this fall, I saw numerous young cedars sprouting in northern forests. Baby balsam and spruce are appearing in large numbers in our woods along the creek. Once over-browsed woodland understories are making a comeback.

Soon, our home along the creek will be the destination for relatives joining us for opening weekend. And when my head hits the pillow on the eve of the annual deer hunt, I will most likely sleep like a log – hoping dreams drift back in time to 1969, when my dear departed dad and I began this journey. To a time when the hunt caused anxiety, stomach pains and a sense of wonderment.

Kinda like falling in love. I thought you might understand.

*****

While the Pilgrims prepared their first Thanksgiving meal, Native American dinner guests arrived bearing five freshly killed deer. Besides venison, the colonists also provided wild fowl including geese, ducks and turkey for the feast. Dinner for 140 required a lot of food and the addition of fish, lobster, clams, nuts, wheat flour and vegetables such as pumpkin, squash, carrots, and peas was necessary.

When our tribe travels over the river and through the woods to grandmother's house this Thanksgiving, the menu will not include fresh venison – as our deer camp has not pulled the trigger as of mid-week. But turkey and duck, sweet and mashed potatoes and gravy, bread stuffing, fresh salad, pumpkin and pecan pie, olives and pickles will all be on the menu.

After dinner, deer hunting stories will be told by the hunters while the rest of the family is entertained by the holiday football game. Somewhere in between, I will nod off, as blood leaves my brain to work on a belly full of food. Thanksgiving afternoon is a traditional day off from hunting, but no doubt my mind will wander back to earlier this week and to the sights, sounds and time standing still on a deer stand.

Heavy fog and standing corn blocked the view from my perch on opening morning. I was not alone, as many hunters across the state found themselves in the same boat. The only deer I saw that first day materialized out of the mist and munched contently on corn twenty yards from my stand. His "nubbin" antlers, barely protruding from his forehead promised the world better things to come.

Engulfed in the haze, I relied on my sense of hearing to tell the story. Two neighbors, both named Jim, connected on bucks that first day. Their shots told the tale, as I knew exactly where their deer stands were located – one to the northeast – the other to the southeast. Additional gunfire was sporadic and noticeably less than normal. I marveled as one shot, a mile to the north, echoed down the river valley and through the dense fog, then bounced back to my ears from a half mile south.

After day one, I saw a couple of does and a spike buck with only one antler. On day four, I did a bit of soul searching when a small eight-point buck stood broadside to my stand by the creek for five minutes. His rack of antlers stretched just shy of ear width – earning him a chance to see another season. There was a time when I would not have thought twice about shooting, but for the past several seasons have passed by a half dozen small bucks, as the boys and I join some of the neighbors practicing trophy buck management. The results are evident as the size and number of larger bucks roaming our woods has increased dramatically.

Neighbors Steve and Brian stopped by our place to compare notes mid-season and echoed the story of unusual low number of deer seen and taken. But a few nice bucks were harvested, including those of Brian's brother Kevin and two neighbors, both named Jim. And so goes another season.

FOOD FOR THE SOUL

November means many things to many people.

For those of us that live north of the tension zone, it represents a transition from warm weather to cold – from daylight savings to standard time – from rainbow colors to drab. However, to the hunter, November – despite the changes – remains food for the soul.

This year, I had trouble letting go of October. The color change alone was bittersweet and the time change occurred way too soon for my internal clock. My beloved woodcock, for the most part, have abandoned the alder bottoms and popple uplands for warmer climates.

Hunters, in general, love yellow leaves and brown grass. If seasons of the year were honored with flags, the colors yellow and brown would be on autumn's banner. Hunters, given the chance, would fly their colors year-round – if only in their dreams – despite the heat, snow, greens and grays of other seasons.

Perhaps that explains the year-round popularity of camouflage clothing on Main Street.

This hunter hates mowing the green grass of summer. During that time of year, I pray for dry spells, hoping the lawn slows down and turns brown. If only summer hours passed by as fast as grass grows, time between Novembers would seem much shorter.

November ultimately puts grass to sleep, while its winds strip trees of any remaining leaves.

The thought of raking leaves when fall winds blow, is also disconcerting to me. Living in the country has allowed me to neglect this annual chore over the years. The lack of neighbors downwind allows nature to do the work for me. Leaves that remain scattered around the yard disappear under the snow and by spring thaw, become food for next year's lawn.

November is forgiving. Other chores, much to the dismay of the boss, remain on the shelf. Precious vacation time, preserved for the hunting season, becomes a priority. Time, unlike "to do" lists, slips away and cannot be posted on the refrigerator for future reference.

The winds of November came in like a lion this time around the sun, knocking at our door with a hint of winter's vengeance. Wind advisories, a chance of snow flurries and shorter days made the transition a bit of a shock.

Suddenly, thanks to the end of daylight saving time, we have reverted to standard time and the length of our days has been artificially shortened – a week later than normal. An energy policy act was signed by the President a few years ago that allows Congress to experiment with the impact of changing the time change dates on our energy need's behalf.

I envy wildlife. Legislated day length means nothing to them. Their clocks are ruled by the sun.

On a recent weekend, relatives visited and our deer stands were inspected and improvements made for the upcoming deer gun hunt. During the week, I'll travel far upstream to hunt grouse near a friend's north woods cabin. Bare trees and the season's first winter storm warning should make for interesting going. Gathering together with friends holding common outdoor passions should make for good times.

November is good for the soul.

*****

"Gotta eat, or you're gonna die!"

That is exactly what the old man wielding a full shopping cart and a large smile exclaimed as we came face-to-face at the local grocery store.

When you are on top of nature's food chain, you hold all the cards. Humans have the ability to pick and choose what they eat and from the beginning of time, that included meat, vegetables and fruit. Every time we eat, something must die. Even true vegetarians are ultimately responsible for the death of thousands of insects – both crawling and flying – as well as small mammals and nesting birds, which die each time heavy farm equipment plows, plants and harvests. That is the price we pay to produce the food we eat – the price we pay to survive. "Gotta eat, or you're gonna die!"

Humans raise livestock and grow crops to fill a craving for fast food, slow food and everything in-between. Some folks are attached by umbilical cord to grocery stores and restaurants. Others hunt, fish and gather to contribute to the dinner table. Our family does both. A good portion of what our boys were weaned on was venison, game birds and fish. Now that they are all but on their own, their personal refrigerators and freezers are full of wild fish and game.

Personally, I love to eat – and about every four to five hours, my furnace cries out to be fed. When you are on the peak of nature's food chain, you control your own dietary destiny. Only once, did the role of sitting on top slip into neutral for me, as I gazed into the eyes of a mother black bear, while she and her cubs came out of winter's hibernation. Luckily, her winter slumber still controlled her mobility and I walked away in one piece with a couple of pictures and a head full of memories.

Our need to eat pales in comparison to the drive wildlife has to feed. Our freeloading songbirds visit the feeders non-stop throughout the day. Deer emerge from the woods several times a day – while chewing their cud – to graze for hours in our soybean food plot. Waterfowl on the neighbor's backwater slough seem to dabble and consume aquatic vegetation and acorns from dawn to dusk. The only creatures that appear to pause between bites are the four-legged and winged predators – on a constant prowl for their next meal.

Creatures of the wild survive from day to day, hour by hour and minute by minute following three simple rules – sleep, eat and procreate. In addition, they are constantly on the alert for danger and continually eyeing their human neighbors. Have you ever pondered on the multitude of perils wildlife face? Life expectancy for wild animals is short and just making it through a typical day can be difficult.

Like young rabbits, potential victims of an owl's wrath while dancing on the lawn in the moonlight. Or, neighbor Larry's sandhill cranes, who together, stand lonely in the mowed hay field, chickless after two disastrous summers. At least three, maybe four young chicks were lost to predators over the course of two breeding seasons. Ground nesting birds of all stripes, like ruffed grouse, woodcock, killdeer and mallards face immense challenges surviving nesting and brooding seasons.

Last summer, I noticed a shortage of turkey broods around our place. Hungry predators take out nests and young of the year – and once again, a family of fishers and several packs of coyotes have been active in the neighborhood. Last spring, I spotted a large fisher with a turkey egg in his mouth running along the edge of a cornfield. He stopped long enough to show off his prize and then hightailed it to the den to feed its young. Overall, there still is a large population of turkeys. Just imagine, without the presence of predators, we would be up to our eyeballs in toms and hens.

Such is the balance of nature and as the saying goes, "Gotta eat, or you're gonna die!"

OF BIRDS AND MEN

There are a few things in nature that take my breath away. Birds in flight are on top of that list. I marvel at their style and grace as they fly by and wonder how they manage the feat. Who among us has not contemplated what it would be like to fly?

Seemingly lighter than air, a bird in the hand weighs little of nothing. Hollow bones and weightless feathers account for next to nothing. The aerobatic hummingbird weighs only 3 grams and flies like a helicopter, flapping its wings at a rate of 70 times per second!

On the other end of the spectrum, cranes, with eight foot wingspans, beat theirs less than once per second. Painting a mental image with words worthy of this magnificent bird is not an easy task. If I were an artist, they would no doubt grace my canvas. To my eye, their outer primaries resemble fingers, feeling their way across the sky.

With wings cupped and webbed feet braced, a flock of geese coming in for a landing can make a grown man look for cover. Hawks and owls fly in silence, hunting day and night respectively. During late summer days, nighthawks zigzag just above the treetops – fueling their bellies with insects as they migrate south.

Eagles soar below the clouds, seemingly without effort, catching the waves of updraft winds. Who cannot resist watching as our national symbol passes by? And who has not imaged hitching a ride as they glide up and down the river valley?

Man's early attempts to fly involved gliders, balloons and powered aircraft. In 1903, the Wright brothers made the first sustained and controlled heavier-than-air powered flight. The rest, as they say, is history. The urge to fly in a plane has never been strong for me. In fact, I avoided flying like the plague, until my real job demanded I use airplanes to travel cross country. My preferred mode of transportation remains four wheels on the pavement and looking at the sky through a moon roof.

The other side of the coin finds No. 2 son embracing flying with a passion. As a toddler, he would point by the kitchen window and cry out, "Airplane-plane, Airplane – plane!" At the tender age of 13, he began flying lessons at a nearby municipal airport. The "boss" and I would hold our breath and watch from the parking lot as he and his flight instructor would take off, disappear over the horizon and return an hour or so later. Then the day came – even before he earned a driver's license – when he flew a plane solo.

After a hiatus of a few years, he's back in the cockpit – on track to earn his pilot license and bring home his wings, so to speak. Then, who knows, perhaps the "boss" and I will hitch a ride as he glides up and down the river valley with the eagles.

THE PRAIRIE

Once upon a time, I had the pleasure of observing the release of several prairie chickens on the Buena Vista Grasslands south of Plover, 30 miles south of our place along the creek. Transplants from northwest Minnesota, the birds were liberated in an effort to strengthen the gene pool of a small, isolated flock. Named a state threatened species in 1979, it is hoped that the new blood will insure their future, as they number less than a few thousand birds in this central part of the state.

Chances are when you think about endangered habitat, wetlands come to mind. But in fact, grasslands are the most endangered vegetative ecosystem in Wisconsin these days. Restoring and maintaining grasslands for wildlife is the driving force behind several groups, including the Central Wisconsin Grassland Conservation Area (CWCGA) Partnership. This partnership project covers portions of six counties, including: Taylor, Clark, Marathon, Portage, Wood and Adams. With an eye towards restoring and creating habitat for grassland species, their ultimate goal is to maintain an open, uninterrupted farm and grassland landscape across the central part of the state.

Wisconsin's native prairies once covered approximately 2.1 million acres – at present, less than 2,500 acres remain. Agricultural conversion over the years to grass hay, small grains and permanent pasture took a toll on wildlife associated with prairies. More than ever, prairies and other grassland habitat – including agricultural hayfields and converted croplands – need to be established, managed and preserved.

Everyone should own a piece of prairie. Whether measured in square feet, acres, or square miles, it matters not. Possessing a piece of prairie gives a person ownership in the past – a window into a land's history. Folks in town plant prairie grasses and wildflowers in small patches, as a bit of landscaping or borders for their backyards. Our prairie along the creek, a work in progress, measures eight acres.

In 2004, number one son brought home a plan for our land sponsored by a local chapter of Pheasants Forever (PF). Dubbed the "habitat organization", this conservation group puts money it raises to good use on the land. Since 1982, their wildlife habitat projects have benefited more than 4 million acres across the U.S. Local chapters sponsor area projects that promote grassland management.

Our project began with burning, treatment and planting. We burned the about half the field that spring with a PF volunteer crew under a permit issued by DNR fire control. After that, we waited until the field "greened up" – then applied an herbicide to remove any undesirable cool-season grasses that survived. Then we planted a warm season prairie grass mix with a neighbor's no-till planter over the burn and old corn stubble that remained on the lower portion of the field.

The grasses planted were Indian grass, switch grass and big and little bluestem. There were five forbs (wildflowers) in the mix and today we see black-eyed Susan and yellow coneflower. In addition, we supplemented with lead plant, butterfly weed, wild Indigo, wild lupine, dotted mint, round-headed bush clover and blazing star – but so far, the only ones we know are growing are the Indigo, lupine and dotted mint. Establishing a diverse prairie takes time and patience.

In order to thrive, prairie grasslands need periodic disturbance. Before disappearing under the plow, grassland wildfires swept across the oceans of grasses because of natural or man-made reasons. Today, maintenance is accomplished by controlled burning, grazing and mowing. Our project is into its fourth year and maintenance is now in order. This summer's work included mowing and grazing half of the field. Next spring we'll burn the rest.

Obligate grassland species – a term used by ornithologists – describes species that require relatively treeless grasslands for most or all parts of their breeding cycles, including nesting and foraging. Loss of contiguous grasslands in Wisconsin has resulted in a decline in certain species that depend on this critical habitat. That's where the CWCGA project steps up to the plate. Their goal is to promote grassland conservation and maintain an open, undeveloped landscape where farming is the major land use.

Common visitors to our field include blackbirds, bluebirds, kingbirds, swallows, sparrows, grackles and goldfinches. I can't remember the last time I've seen a meadowlark or bobolink in our field.

With a little luck, our little prairie may someday attract them back. Stay tuned.

WOODCOCK HEAVEN

I've been thinking a lot about Heaven this fall. Not because I spent the better part of a week in the great northwoods hunting ruffed grouse with Pastor Craig. Nor did it have anything to do with a regularly scheduled check-up with Dr. Dean. Despite courageous attempts, neither man put the fear of God in me. No, my brush with thoughts from beyond came at the hands of a piece of land.

It's a special place I have visited each fall for more than four decades. A location that harbors the upland birds my dogs and I love to hunt. Early on, I shot a whitetail buck or two there during deer season – but it is woodcock and grouse, dogwood, willow and aspen that bring me back, year after year. A destination that I'm so fond of, I call it "Woodcock Heaven".

Now with all due respect, I have no illusion that this special place compares to the real thing – in fact, it must pale in comparison. But for this believer, my little slice of paradise has become a window of sorts, revealing better things to come.

When we spend time together in autumn, Pastor Craig and I have wonderful conversations about things of nature and religion. We talk of creatures, great and small, and of people, wise and otherwise. We pondered such things as, "Do dogs go to heaven?" While at the seminary a few years ago, he posed that very question to a nationally-known, traveling theologian. His reply, "As a matter of fact, after much contemplation, I have

110

concluded that they and all of God's creations will be with us in the hereafter."

With that in mind, the landscape in paradise must resemble special places we know on earth. Pastor Craig assured me it's everything good we know on earth and much, much more. Our Woodcock Heaven is an oasis in an ocean of grassland and cultivated fields. Forty acres of aspen and dogwood groomed by owner and good friend Mike, for woodcock, grouse and a host of other critters that also call it home. For more than four decades we have crisscrossed its borders and penetrated its core. Mike asked me this fall while hunting to guess how many times we had walked its trails together over the years. More than we could fathom, I surmised. Then I counted the ghosts of bird dogs we have followed in the process and sighed.

And when I paused to let a flushed woodcock fly off unmolested, I smiled and gave thanks for this special place that gives me pause to ponder each fall. A piece of land that bears the fruits of friendship and nature's bounties. A place I call Woodcock Heaven. A place I hope to share for many years to come.

Thanks Mike.

DEAR DOCTOR DEAN

Dear Dr. Dean,
I realize this report on my health is two months premature, but I had an inspiration to drop you a note just the same – so as not to bore you with all the following details during my next regularly scheduled checkup in November.

As a sportsman in your own right, you, of all people should know the medicinal value of participating in outdoor sports. Now that fall is upon us, I honestly hope you play hooky from the clinic on occasion, secretly toss a fly or two for trout, or grab your musky rod to hunt for yet another elusive 50-incher before the water turns to ice.

In my case, the urge to follow bird dogs in October began in early September. No. 2 son and I went up north for the ruffed grouse opener. Despite mid-day heat, abundant bear hunters, mosquitoes and heavy foliage, the dogs enjoyed the cool, early morning temperatures and dew on the grasses and ferns. We didn't see or hear any birds at the first two coverts, but hit a "mother-lode" at a third location, where No. 2 got a good dose of humility as the first bird of the year sailed unscathed and slow-motion down a logging road. All I heard was "Click" and "What the heck!" after he realized his gun was unloaded.

We split up two coveys of grouse totaling at least nine birds on that walk, missed twice and came back to the truck sweating, scratching, but smiling. We were exactly where we wanted to be and couldn't be happier.

112

So, beginning this month a regular dose of exercise is on my agenda – cardiovascular in nature – beginning on the weekends, then after work occasionally during the week. Come October, my stockpiled vacation time will be cashed in and the dogs and I will be "working out" daily. Where this hunter's road leads in October remains to be seen. November will bring the nine-day deer season, December late season ruffed grouse, and January promises a trip to the western prairies – home to abundant pheasants, quail and prairie chickens.

My blood pressure is beginning to drop just thinking about it. All other vital signs appear stable. My appetite is fine, yet I should lose a pound or two along the way. By the end of the season, I should be fit as a fiddle.

Author Havilah Babcock, in his book, My Health is Better in November, described a hunter's overall wellbeing as follows; "Outdoor pursuits have a therapeutic value, a stirring day in the field purges the mind. When the first frost comes, there is a noticeable improvement in his health."

So, by the time I see you in November I ought to pass your examination with flying colors. Better yet, why don't we just postpone my appointment a few months? By mid-January, I should be back from the prairies and in pretty good shape – for the shape I'm in.

Yours in good health,
Ken

SOLUNAR

Have you ever wondered if you are in the right place at the right time?

As far as hunting, fishing and even bird watching goes, timing can be critical. Forecasting the times of day and night when fish and game are most active is not only possible, it has been studied and documented for decades. The results are at our fingertips – thanks to a very clever fellow, the sun and the moon.

In 1926, outdoor writer, fisherman and hunter John Alden Knight, studied relentlessly the factors which influenced or controlled the day-to-day behavior of fish and game. Beginning with moon, tide and barometric theories and knowing that critters tend to feed actively during sunrise and sunset, he eventually concentrated on the effect of moonrise and moonset, as well as new and full moons. He threw in a dash of the sun and weather's influence – a calendar and a clock, and thus, the famous Solunar Tables were born.

Did you know that moonrise can occur at any time during the day or night? When that coincides with a sunrise or sunset, major fish and game activity occurs. Add a full moon and watch out! Minor, intermediate activity periods also occurs midway between two major periods. Every day of the year, four times a day – critical moments have been identified and worth observation.

John Alden Knight formulated and first published his tables in 1936. Following in his father's footsteps, Richard Alden Knight continued to put the charts to print and today Solunar Tables can be found in 110 newspapers and the nationally published monthly magazine, *Field & Stream*. You can account for your home geographic location and time zone – adjust for daylight savings and then determine the best times to hunt, fish or simply observe.

If the force of the moon can move oceans with its gravitational pull, surely it can influence not only animals and fish – but man. Some say full and new moons can manipulate personality traits such as creativity and spirituality, as well as a person's mood and behavior. It is said that full moons can cause stress, sensitivity to details and a general lack of assertiveness. New moons bring back calmness, normal emotions, energy and a sense of accomplishment. Perhaps Knight's tables can also be used to predict moments of the day that will prove to be most productive for mankind.

So, for the rest of this year and into next, I will watch Knight's Solunar Tables afield, at work and at home. Will I find more ruffed grouse feeding along the trails at 5:30 pm on opening day? Will migrant woodcock actively follow the Harvest Moon in October? What time of day will buck deer be most active during the early November rut? Best time to fish? And what about scheduling the next family gathering or work related staff meeting around the moon and the sun?

I wonder if Mr. Knight, back in 1936, dreamed he'd still have the attention of folks in the year 2012? He certainly has mine.

Winter

"As I passed by a stand of hemlocks, I gazed towards the upper branches and there he was – my roosting grouse, silhouetted against the fading light."

TRACKS IN THE SNOW

A track in the snow tells no lies. That fact was evident on a recent trek along the creek and soon after a fresh snowfall. It all began when the boss spotted a lone tom turkey out the kitchen window. Through the spotting scope I saw his enormous beard, dangling in the snow. He pecked his way slowly along the edge of our food plot, where it joins the banks of a frozen pond. His presence and a fresh snowfall lured me outside despite the bitter cold wind out of the north.

I followed his tracks and surveyed the virgin blanket of snow up and down the creek. At first, I crossed the path of a pair of foxes, able to stroll atop the harden layer of snow that measured eleven inches on the level. With a crust at two inches below the surface, their light weight – 10 pounds, give or take a few – allowed for smooth sailing as they hunted for their next meal. They lingered a while under our little red pine plantation, a place where rabbit tracks abound. With nothing but footprints to sniff, they took to the creek bottom and headed west.

Then I met the tracks of turkeys – by my count, four individual birds – on their way from feeding in the neighbor's picked cornfield to an acorn crop and evening roost in the woods. The lone tom that we saw earlier had split off from the group, only to meet up later on the trail along the creek.

After crossing the creek near our line fence, an abundance of deer tracks appeared – in stark contrast to their absence in our

119

fields. Fifty yards into the woods, I came face-to-face to a large doe and her triplet fawns. Were they the same family group we observed all summer long in our food plot? If so, that answered the question of survival during the recent deer hunt.

I carried a camera instead of a gun that day – hanging up my urge to "earn a buck" by shooting a doe as a credit for next season. Just as well – pulling the trigger would have tested my will to shoot a doe this late in the year. I will take care of that issue next year, should the state sentence our zone to the next level of herd management.

I passed by as the four stood frozen in their tracks – akin to concrete yard statues – never taking their eyes off my progress. Then, in an instance, a small buck materialized out of nowhere, jumping over the trail near the southeast corner of the forty – disappearing into the neighboring woods faster than he appeared. His tracks in the snow painted a picture of flight, the distance between hoof prints measured in yards rather than feet or inches.

Turning to the north, then west, I crossed paths with a set of tracks left by a ruffed grouse. A loner in the pines, never on the ground longer than five, or six feet – then taking flight to low branches bearing buds – a winter staple of grouse diet. Then suddenly, any sign of his whereabouts disappeared. Where did he go?

It was late in the afternoon when I emerged from the woods on the blacktopped road that borders the west side of our property. As I passed by a stand of hemlocks, I gazed towards the upper branches and there he was – my roosting grouse, silhouetted against the fading light.

Tracks in the snow tell no lies – but convey a good story to those who take the time to read them.

120

CHRISTMAS POWER OUTAGE

Like many other folks, we were caught a bit off guard during the power outage that hit the river valley one past Christmas weekend. Life in the country has its distinct advantages, except when the electric meter stops spinning, the lights go out and the "well goes dry". Not literally, but without power, the pump won't run and the well sits idle. Our urban neighbors are at an advantage, because community water systems are designed to provide continuous service during blackouts, relying on elevated storage and standby auxiliary power.

With luck, we thought as we turned in for the night, electrical service would back by sunrise. Wrong! Eight hours into the outage and two hours before it got light, the boss woke up and began to inventory our candle supply. Her sleep was interrupted by the nagging thought of her day devoted to holiday preparation being sabotaged. Baking, cooking and cleaning were in jeopardy and with a houseful of guests due to arrive on Sunday, she was getting nervous. So, it was at the kitchen table in the candlelight that I found her and it was there that we contemplated our options.

The burners on the LP gas stove still worked, so melting snow with which to fill the tanks on the toilets for flushing was doable. A few bottles of drinking water from the fridge made perking coffee on the stove possible. Those first cups in the morning sure tasted good and made waking up in a "cool" house easier. Without wood heat that year, we were at the mercy of milder than normal winter temperatures. Sixty-two degrees wasn't too bad when wearing a sweatshirt.

A battery-powered radio was our link to the outside world. If nothing else, the noise broke the silence and music soothed the nerves. Television was out of the question and in fact, its absence was a pleasant diversion. I've often felt that if a person's status in life is judged by size of their big screen television, then our family could be labeled rich beyond belief. Not only do we own one, but two units grace our residence – one upstairs and the other below. Both are solar powered and require no electricity. The upper level one measures 5 x 7 feet – the lower 4 x 8 feet. Together, they provide nearly 70 square of viewing pleasure to the outside natural world beyond the confines of our home. One's a kitchen picture window, the other a French-style doorway in the master bedroom. We wake each morning to an easterly view of our field and woods. Birdfeeders outside both windows bring literally hundreds of hours of wholesome performances from a wide cast of characters. It was there we found ourselves as the sun came up ten hours into the power outage. Oblivious to the trouble their landlords were having, the resident flock of songbirds gave a performance fit for a king. First the cardinal gang came, including seven bright red males followed by their mates and an assortment of blue jays, chickadees, juncos, nuthatches, sparrows, doves, goldfinches and woodpeckers.

Cooking chores might have begun with a loaf of bread, had I remembered to pick one up the day before. You see, real family-style Swedish meatballs are browned on the stove and made with ground venison, bread and other secret ingredients. So, after calling to see if they were open for business, it was my job to drive to the store in town at hour fourteen. On my way home, I ran into some neighbors and together we caught glimpses of electric utility repair trucks in the area. Could relief be far off?

By the sixteenth hour, the power company announced that for some, liberation might not occur until Christmas Eve. It was time for extreme action and by then we were ready to hook-up a large generator to run the pump and furnace. A neighbor stopped by within minutes of firing up the beast and reported that power restoration was just minutes away – and sure enough, after nearly nineteen hours, power was back! A full-course press to ready the house for Christmas guests was now possible.

For some we're told, the predicament stretched on. I guess we were on the list of lucky customers. Unfortunately for the power company, they must have taken a good financial hit, given the scope and expense of this major outage. They'll survive, as rate adjustments will take care of that. But our heart-felt thanks go out to the utility crews and office folks that worked night and day throughout the holidays, missing their own family celebrations – so that we could enjoy the time spent with our family and friends.

"CHICK-A-DEE-DEE-DEE"

Of all the birds that frequent our feeders, it's the Black-capped Chickadees that steal the show for me. Collectively, the colorful portrait outside our kitchen window includes more dramatic red male cardinals, rowdy blue jays and black, white and sometimes red woodpeckers. But hands down, my favorite bird is the Chickadee – a feathered friend that years ago, led me to two most interesting fellows.

Bold by nature, these small, energetic birds are about 5 inches long, black capped, black bibbed and sport a pair of white cheeks. For those with time and patience, they can be persuaded to take a sunflower seed from an extended hand. Interesting fellow number one taught me how. He was the grandfather of friend Ron and lived in the north woods near Monico.

"Grandpa" had a flock of tame Chickadees working his living room window feeder and he was proud to show them off. He spoke of them with delight, as he did the flying squirrels that visited each evening – the spotlight we bought had brought them closer to his world. During the day, with nothing but time on his hands, he had patiently conditioned his birds to feed from hand. The secret to his success involved cracking the sunflower shells and exposing the edible kernel. He insisted, "Take a handful and try for yourself."

To experience a living creature weighing 1/3 of an ounce balance weightlessly on your hand, is to appreciate the saying, "lighter than air". The birds that dared to eat from my hand that day did so with gusto, as the prediction for cold temperatures were in the forecast. When temperatures drop to zero degrees Fahrenheit the Chickadee must consume up to 60% of its body weight in food. For a person weighing 200 pounds, that would translate into nearly 120 pounds of groceries!

Away from the birdfeeders and deep in the woods, a Chickadee's diet consists of insects, insect eggs, spiders, spider eggs, berries and small seeds from pine cones. During the cold months of winter, they locate hidden food they've stored under the bark and cracks of trees and branches deep in the woods. That's where I met fellow number two – the late, great ornithologist, Don "Fuzz" Follen of Arpin.

Back in the early 1980's, Don literally took me by the hand and led me deeper into the wonderful world of birds and bird banding. I followed him across flowages to band osprey, up trees to band several species of owls and even across the state to find the elusive Great Gray owl. Don taught me to question the unknown and his home in the swamp was a perfect setting for exploring nature's mysteries. From his window one day, he pondered after watching a steady flow of Chickadees coming to his feeders, "There's no way the same birds are eating all the sunflower seeds we put out."

So, he started an aggressive banding program that would count and mark the birds, one at a time. He gave up after tagging well over a hundred birds, noting that they must come and go from long distances to his feeding station. They didn't all belong to his backyard flock. As it turned out, Don had experienced a major fall chickadee flight – a minor invasion which established the winter territories of the birds near his home on the edge of a rather large swamp.

Our feeders along the creek aren't an attraction for a flight of these tiny bundles of energy, but we get our share. Time and patience aren't in the cards these days, but some day, not too far around the corner, I plan on cracking some seeds and handing out a few kernels to the willing. And all I'll ask in return is a few cheerful "chick-a-dee-dees".

COUNTING SNOWFLAKES

It started with a single snowflake. One flake followed by another and yet another, until a mountain of flakes became a blanket. A blanket of snow – that for the most part, has made many folks around here weary of winter. Last Sunday's snowfall stopped most of us in our tracks – enough already!

Record snowfalls pile up across the state, with no end in sight. Our memory of the winter of 2008 will not fade away any time soon. No matter where you turn, snow is on everyone's mind. The total depth in Fond du Lac this season is 80 inches and last weekend's storm shattered their nearly 80-year old record. Madison accumulated 87 inches of snow to-date, 50 inches above normal. Here along our stretch of the Wisconsin River valley, nearly 60 inches has fallen – far short of a 1922 high of more than 80 inches – but one for the record book nonetheless.

Although it's a curse for those nursing sore backs and wielding snow shovels, abundant snow is in fact a blessing in disguise. In short order, warmer temperatures will turn feet of snow cover into much needed inches of groundwater – as parched aquifers await a fresh supply of water that avoids running off downstream during the melt. Several years of drought conditions have lowered lake levels, slowed stream flows and rendered water tables weak. Perhaps the drought has turned a corner and an increase in precipitation will now be the rule – snowflake by snowflake, raindrop by raindrop.

Individual snowflakes, when put under a microscope, bring the world of art and science into concert. To view a single snowflake – and for that matter, designs made by frost on windowpanes – is to draw the observer into another dimension. To count a billion snowflakes would be laborious.

In 1880, fifteen-year-old Vermont farmer Wilson Bentley, drew pictures of his "tiny miracles of beauty" – snowflakes. By age twenty, he had devised a method to catch flakes on velvet cloth and photograph their image before they melted. Over a lifetime, he recorded over 5,000 different ice crystal shapes. He long contended that no two snowflakes were alike, each with a unique design and shape. He went on to photograph other forms of water – like ice, raindrops, clouds and fog.

Wilson "Snowflake" Bentley died a single man. Just as well, a woman married to a man whose passion was counting snowflakes would surely have suffered. Mixing the incredible complexity of nature, crystalline science and snowflake art – his legacy brought science and art together, answering yet another piece of nature's puzzle.

Stepping beyond science, we can only grin and bear it and embrace nature's way. As the snow melts next month, recall the unpredictability and power of Mother Nature and prepare for flooding, as it is likely to follow. For those that live in heavy soils and low-lying areas – make sure your sump pump is in good working order.

WINTER GROUSE HUNTS

Hunting ruffed grouse during winter months is not for the faint of heart.

For the past several years, minimal snow cover has afforded hunters and their bird dogs smooth going – but this season's abundant snowfall is reason enough to put a damper on grouse hunting – a favorite pastime for northern upland bird hunters.

Strolling along colorful game trails in October seems a distant memory when snow depths range from 8 to 16 inches, north and south. It looks like a good, old-fashioned Wisconsin winter is upon us. The white stuff – drifting knee-deep in places – has all but turned away even the heartiest of bird hunters.

On the other hand, with deep, powdery snow for night roosting, grouse are in winter heaven. Their habit of roosting in the upper reaches of pines has suddenly been abandoned for more favorable snow roosts – a behavior that conserves energy and contributes to better over-winter survival.

When I was twenty-something, my buddies and I would put on our felted-lined, rubber bottomed boots and wade through knee-deep snow. Subsequently, at thirty and forty-something, I slowed down considerably, but would occasionally strap on my snowshoes and head for the tag-alder edged swamps. This winter, at fifty-something, I was put to the test once again. Two weekends ago, a close friend and hunting buddy, Dale dropped by and we trudged through the season's first snowfall, which, after a bit of rain, left about eight inches of wet, crusty snow. We managed a mile and a half swing through the woods and in the process Dale – much to both of our delights – put a brace of grouse in the bag.

A planned outing with several good friends this weekend will include snowshoes, but appears to be eroding into a combination hunt and ice-fishing excursion. This annual end-of-the-year tradition typically encompassed hunts an hour north and an hour south of our place. Last year, we encountered snow up north, but bare, November-like conditions to the south.

Three things I most love about this time of the year are late-season grouse hunting, old dogs and cold, finger-numbing winter days in the woods. I hope to spend a bit of time with all three next month. The dogs and I will explore the woods close to home, searching for wintering ruffed grouse. Together, we will hunt on paper mill land, state wildlife management areas and on property along the Wisconsin River bottoms.

Snowshoes will be in order, as the knee-deep snow can be a real chore for an aging hunter. During those hunts – if history repeats itself – I will take a couple of spills while traversing the cattail marshes along frozen backwater sloughs. Falling on snowshoes in deep snow is easy. Getting back up is another matter. Using my gun for support, after unloading, I'll get back on my feet and head for frozen backwater sloughs and beaver ponds. There, the snow isn't as deep and makes for easier going.

Grouse hunting after the snow gets deep is often a labor of love. And that's why hunting "old ruff" in January trips my trigger. It makes hunting grouse the following year in October that much more enjoyable.

Hunting with an old bird dog is just plain satisfying and hours spent are quality time for sure. Each hunt could be their last, but there's always hope for just one more season together.

Finger-numbing days? Well, knowing there's a warm truck and home to go back to at the end of the day helps. And the long, cold winter gives us pause to dream about spring, summer and fall.

*****

Ruffed grouse hunting along the creek spans two seasons.

Gone are the golden days of autumn, as lush foliage has been replaced by snow, naked trees and chill arctic winds. Walking takes on new meaning when snow reaches the top of one's boots – no longer are hunts a casual stroll through the woods. Grouse have taken to sleeping in snow banks and feeding on the sly, early and late in the day. To do otherwise would likely prove fatal.

Most upland hunters have stored their shotguns, some long before the first snowflakes hit the ground. The few that persist have given up their light vests, jackets and rubber boots for heavy wool, fleece and hooded parkas. Long underwear and insulated boots are now the rule.

It has become a family tradition, our winter holiday ruffed grouse hunts. And ever since No. 1 son went out-of-state for a higher education, has become a homecoming event of sorts. A regular holiday ritual, standing the test of time.

This year is no exception.

On the first Monday, the boys and I visited a cover we call the Railroad Crossing that borders a black spruce and tamarack bog. For some reason, grouse gather there in December and since discovering their hideout, we pay them at least one visit each season. While working the bog's snow covered alder edge the boys and their dog named Sue moved five grouse, one of which fell to No. 1's gun. A half hour later, we checked a place labeled Six Mile, which yielded not a single flush, but afforded another brisk

131

walk in ankle-deep snow while our dogs Rocky and Sue enjoyed one more chance to stretch their legs.

On Tuesday, we visited a location closer to home by a neighbor's beaver pond, dubbed the Mother Cover. We worked its length, almost a quarter mile long, without success. Not until we explored an adjacent cover bordering a picked cornfield did we see a single bird that offered no shot. Next on our agenda was an old standby near the Phantom Grouse Cover that failed to produce, so we called it a day. That evening, after adding a couple of previously harvested birds from the freezer, our family sat down to a delicious meal of grouse alfredo, prepared by No. 1 son.

Wednesday morning dawned with an eastern red sky and the promise of another major snowstorm. After chores around the house, we snuck off to several other spots close at hand. But that was after this column's deadline, so all I can promise is a vision of what might have been.

With luck, after Christmas, the boys and I will connect with several close friends for another holiday habit, a New Year's grouse hunt in Lincoln, Wood or Monroe counties with Tim, Rich, their boys and Dale.

As you can see, surrounding myself with family and friends in the woods – is truly a holiday tradition.

THE OTHER HUNTERS

This is a story of a bear, a hawk and a wolf. All three made their presence known along the creek this past weekend and if I was writing a book on the subject, each would easily earn a chapter by themselves. Three tales of hunters, predators and the outdoor world they share.

It began as a few close friends gathered at our place to wrap up the hunting season with a traditional late season ruffed grouse hunt. The search for birds was sidetracked for a moment when good friend Tim and his son Travis followed their German shorthaired pointer, "Hammer" into thick alders. They found him standing rigid only a few feet away from a hibernating black bear! Much to their relief, the dog heeded commands to stay put, while the large bruin rolled out of bed and lumbered off.

Back at headquarters, we feasted on hot chili, soup and sandwiches while matching stories of the day, the year and seasons past. As we sat around the table, not one, but two small birds flew into the kitchen window from our backyard feeders. We jumped up and peered outside at one of the hapless birds lying on the ground, a junco – just in time to see a sharp-shinned hawk swoop in and fly off with the small bird in its talons.

While predator number 2 devoured his prey high in a backyard tree, all other birds scattered to the winds – except one trembling downy woodpecker, who remained plastered to a hanging suet feeder for ten minutes. Only when the other birds returned, did our little woodpecker release his grip and resume feeding.

The last page of this tale began two days later when neighbor Jim dropped by with holiday cheer and a hot tip. Seems his son Brian spotted some wolf tracks in the snow a little more than a half mile as the crow flies from our house. It was garbage day and right after a quick trip to the township garage, I headed to the scene. In short order, I spotted the tracks, as they were exactly where Jim had indicated.

Tracks in the snow tell no lies and when read, told a good story of predator number 3. Out of a marsh came a single set, crossed the road, looped around an ice-covered pond then disappeared once again in the marsh to the south. I drove a mile to the southwest and picked up the wolf's tracks where it crossed another road and disappeared to the west through a marsh bordering a small spruce bog. At one point, I crawled down the ditch bank, took pictures and measured the length of one well-defined track. It reached five and a half inches in length by four inches wide – large by wolf standards, most likely indicating a male.

So, winter may have brought an end to our hunting season, but for our neighborhood predators, the hunt is on and a year-round occupation.

*****

Like a whisper, the pair slipped in and out of our property with little fanfare. They crossed the south fence line silently and under the cover of darkness. The light crunch of their paws on crusty snow was perhaps the only sound they made.

A pair of wolves passed through our "forty" last Friday night.

On Saturday morning, the tracks they left were still fresh.

Backtracking was easy, revealing where they entered our property together behind Golden Pond, passing by Uncle Mike's deer stand and finally splitting apart as they coursed a deer bedding area.

The larger male's tracks came out on the field directly east of the house then turned towards Vera's Pond. The smaller female's tracks came out of the woods by our duck blind and crossed the field west of the pond. They met up again by the road and followed a heavily used deer trail that leads into a freshly harvested field of corn to the north.

Our place along the creek lies in Wisconsin's "tension zone", a vegetative transition area dividing southern habitats from the northwoods, and contain many large tamarack/spruce bogs – ideal secluded wolf habitat for denning and hunting. A small herd of deer – numbering ten at last count – have taken to our woods this winter, bedding down during the day, coming out at dusk each evening to feed on corn residue across the road.

The wolves moved quickly across our land, each stride indicating a trot. They passed through the deer bedding area, which was empty that night, then followed a well-used deer trail leading to the corn. It has been determined by experts that the daily movements of wolves are dictated by pack territories – ranging in size from 50 to more than 1,000 square miles. No doubt, central Wisconsin wolves live within the smaller range, yet by nature, and at a five mile per hour trot, they can travel up to 30 miles in a day searching for a meal.

Sightings, tracks and howling have become more common in our neighborhood. To the west, a much larger pack has established itself on a large piece of public land. A network of spruce/tamarack bogs in our township, like islands on a lake, have become stepping stones for overflow members of the larger pack.

I know the thought of wolves puts many folks in a negative

135

mood, but for me, it pulls at something I'm not sure of. Something I know deep down is good. I'm not too concerned that they share our backyard – once and awhile. But you better believe we are on alert when we walk with our birddogs. Wolves are not very tolerant of lesser canines.

A pair of wolves paid a visit last weekend. And while following the tracks backwards, they led me to a grouse budding in an old aspen tree by Golden Pond.

Then on Sunday morning, while at the breakfast table, we spotted our deer herd – still numbering ten – as they came off the corn field, passed by Vera's Pond and returned to their beds under the pines along the creek.

TRAVEL WEST

An extended journey took us two thousand miles west of our place along the creek. You see, No. 1 son became a temporary resident of the state of Nevada – at least for as long as it takes him to earn his doctorate degree in wildlife management.

The trip began on a Sunday, just after sunrise and ended around noon on the following Tuesday. Along the way, we passed through 7 states, crossed over the continental divide, adjusted to three time zones and traveled over, or around 7 mountain ranges. For three amazing days, we left behind our beloved state of Wisconsin and experienced a transformation into another world.

Day one took us through the land of corn, wheat fields, marshes and grasslands – home of pheasant, quail, white-tailed deer and prairie grouse. The Platte River of Nebraska follows Interstate 80 and afforded us a waterfowl show of geese and ducks along the way. The rolling grasslands of western Nebraska replaced the flat terrain of Iowa and eastern Nebraska – leading us to Wyoming's majestic Rocky Mountains at Medicine Bow.

Suddenly, we found ourselves in a land of antelope, mule deer, elk, coyote and eagles. Herds of antelope gathered together along the interstate, struggling to feed in the snow-covered sagebrush. Heavier snows in the upper reaches of the mountains has driven other big game animals to lower elevations – and exposed them to observant passer-bys. We lost track of the number of mule deer seen and in the process, yours truly saw a buck of a lifetime. Enormous elk, victims of the weather, were seen lying dead along the shoulder – impressive road kills indeed.

Signs at every mountain pass bore flashing lights and warnings – calling for mandatory tire chains and four-wheel drive during emergency storm conditions. Gates – capable of barricading an interstate highway in minutes – stood ready for the next winter blizzard. When Mother Nature raises her hackles and dumps mountain snow, the roadway closes down for days on end – until heavy equipment can clear a path.

We snuck through 5 mountain passes and across the continental divide without incident. Travelers the week preceding ours were not so lucky – as a winter storm shut down the interstate and stopped passage. The most hazardous condition we encountered was heavy fog around the Cedar Mountains of Great Salt Lake. As we entered the desert flats beyond the Lake, the fog lifted and it was back to normal cruise control speed.

Our destination state greeted us with mountain range after mountain range. Clouds hovered below the tops of the snow-covered peaks – drawing us from one breath-taking scene to the next. Across the length of Nevada, one never loses sight of the mountains and the ever-present clouds, stretching across the horizon – dancing and skipping – always off to the next mountain top.

We made Reno by noon of the third day – rolling the mileage odometer over two thousand and five times. "The Biggest Little City in the World" is located on the east slope of the Sierra Nevadas and is home for the University of Nevada – Reno. No. 1 son will spend five years studying the impact of man's activities on the greater sage grouse – North America's largest grouse species.

I was awful glad to be in on the ground floor of his voyage.

CHRISTMAS TREES AND REDHEADS

No holiday is more immersed in family traditions than Christmas. Like greeting cards, festive carols, church, get-togethers, meals, decorations, mistletoe, presents and trees – just to name a few. Our family traditions begin with the harvest of a tree along the creek and ends with a ruffed grouse hunt or two. In-between, we hang stockings by the woodstove, gather with family and friends, brew Swedish glogg and consume food – lots of food

For several decades, at the end of deer season, a live evergreen has been selected, cut and decorated to grace our living room. The woods we own harbor a wide variety of conifers, including several varieties of spruce, hemlock, fir, pine and larch. This year, a special spruce found its way into our home and hearts, by way of a story involving a very special whitetail buck.

We planted the spruce as a seedling many years ago. It, along with several others was placed along a trail leading to "Golden Pond" and Uncle Mike's elevated deer stand. When the spruce reached adolescence, a mature buck selected it as a sparring partner – polishing his antlers while rubbing the velvet off his majestic rack of twelve points. Like other bucks of his nature, he chose the small pine as a territorial marker for all others to see. The broken limbs and eight inch "rub" on the lower end of the trunk spoke volumes and its location along the trail stood out like a billboard.

139

That fall, Uncle Mike tagged the buck as it tried to sneak past his stand. It turned out to be his personal best whitetail trophy and now hangs in his home in Rio – bringing back fond memories of another very special family tradition.

In the mean time, the spruce survived. Slightly deformed at the base and missing some branches on one side, it grew straight and strong. Above the scars, it became a handsome tree – and caught my eye again this fall during the deer hunt.

Our Christmas tree harvest ritual, when started so many years ago, meant giving up the hope of displaying a well-groomed conifer, like those which grow on tree farms. Many there are of the non-native variety – ours have been native firs, pine and spruce – shaped as nature intended.

So, if you happen by this holiday season for a visit, or spot our lighted tree through the window, keep in mind, its demise was not in vain. The boss and I planted nearly a hundred in its place last summer – so the tradition can continue for many years to come.

Here's hoping your family holiday traditions all come true.

$$*****$$

They're back. A pair of our favorite backyard woodpeckers has returned after a short hiatus. Perhaps it was it the red that caught my eye through the kitchen window, or the stark contrast of red against a black and white body. Odds are, it was the red feathers wrapping their heads that grabbed my attention.

A deep, potent red that defies description. Deeper, richer than Cardinal red. A scarlet red that puts fire trucks and morning skies for sailors to shame. When Mother Nature passed out the color red, leftovers of lesser shades were given to all others.

Always a crowd pleaser at the feeding station outside our kitchen window, and for as long as I can remember, at least one pair of Red-headed Woodpeckers resided here year-round, consuming our suet in winter and raising a youngster or two each summer.

Wisconsin is home for seven assorted woodpeckers including; the Downy, Hairy, Red-headed, Red-bellied, Pileated, Northern Flicker and Yellow-bellied Sapsucker – all of which have lived by, or visited our place along the creek. All males and most females have at least one thing in common, a dash or more of red on their heads – a woodpecker trademark.

A while back, my mother-in-law called to report a Pileated Woodpecker at their Wautoma suet feeder. Twice the size of its Red-headed cousin, in fact, more Crow-sized, they are our state's largest woodpecker. The ones that live along our creek bottom seldom visit the backyard, preferring the solitude of the woods – drumming on dead elms and carving large oval holes, at times several feet long, in rotting tree trunks.

Their explosive, jungle-like call often reverberates across the river valley, sounding like a laugh and revealing their presence, even when the bird is out of sight. The bright red crest on their heads made them the model for Mel Blanc's character named Woody.

But more often than not, it is our Red-heads that steal the show. Significant, because of alarming news from the Audubon Society's watch list which notes "a 50% population reduction since 1966. The Christmas Bird Count indicates a similar population decline, with both a decrease in the number of individuals recorded and the number of individuals observed per party hour." Of special interest, has been an occasional local population increase associated with healthy beaver populations and "the creation of flooded forests with lots of snags for nesting."

So, if the Audubon folks are looking for a couple of Redheads, or a chance sighting of a Pileated for their Christmas bird count, they ought to swing by our place. Time it right and ours most likely will put on a show.

We'll keep the suet feeders full.

CAMPFIRE CIRCLES

Dreams of summer campfires in the dead of winter draw closer when one stares into a glass door woodstove. Campfires and woodstoves have much in common. Recently, while sitting mesmerized, watching flames dance together behind the glass, I pondered of years around campfires with family and friends.

In life's journey, the circle of friends we keep defines how we act, who we are and what we ultimately become. By all accounts, a person is measured by the company he or she spends time with, day in and day out. Outdoors men and women have many things in common, with close friends and shared passions ranking high on the list. Gather them together around a campfire and a portrait of their lives emerges.

Friends have met in a circle about fires since the beginning of time. Shoulder to shoulder, they sat around the flames to share warmth as well as storytelling, songs, lies, laughter and tears. I fancy that many a world problem has been solved around a campfire. Before television, phones and newspapers, it was a place outdoors folks would get together for entertainment, news and comfort.

Did you ever wonder why a campfire is circular in design? A square fire pit is hardly practical. Round perhaps, since the circle is recognized as a symbol of unity, of infinity, without beginning or end – perfect, the ultimate geometric symbol. It is about equality

– each member receives an equal dose of warmth. And the circle represents matters of nature – the sun, the moon, planets, tree rings, life and death.

Built openly on the ground, fire rings were made of boulders, concrete and metal – designed to contain and embrace, while preventing flames from spreading. Churches should be round, with the altar in the middle. Without backs and sides, the congregation would face the pastor, each other and the Lord. At one time, round barns were constructed to accommodate the farmer – once around the stalls, he would milk, feed and find himself back at the door and closer to his own meal. Circular homes never seemed to catch on – perhaps not enough places to hide – as family members need their space.

Early settlers rested their wagons in a circle around a fire to keep creatures away in the dark of night and desperados at bay when attacked. Small coveys of bobwhite quail and large herds of massive arctic tundra musk ox circle at night or when threatened. Safe, secure and with peace of mind, it is a matter of creature and human comfort to do so.

So, who do you share your campfires with these days? Those that share the campfires of my mind include both living and departed. When the time comes to gather in the hereafter, it will be a grand affair indeed – defying the common belief that Satan has the market on flames.

Until then, if the masses name me king, I will rule that cities, villages and townships mandate campfire rings in every backyard. Just imagine how better off we all would be.

LEOPOLD INSPIRATION

Let there be no mistake, the finest words ever penned on the principled value of burning firewood to heat a home was by Aldo Leopold in his A Sand County Almanac essay, "Good Oak". Thoughtfully he supposed, "If one has cut, split, hauled and piled his own good oak, and let his mind work the while, he will remember much about where the heat comes from – while a February blizzard tosses the trees outside."

He then described the process – from the bolt of lightning that "put an end to wood-making by this particular oak", to laying "a newly filed saw to its bastioned base – on a crisp winter's day". His brilliant essay then takes the reader on a historical journey, as the saw blade cuts through a century of growth rings – "stroke by stroke, decade by decade, into a chronology of a lifetime, written in concentric annual rings of good oak."

I read the essay each year, about this time to remind myself of the worth of wood as fuel. Back in the 1940s, the Leopold family used saws with teeth to make "a split of good oak for the andirons". These days, a saw with chains is the tool of choice. But the end product is the same – firewood. Now classified a biofuel, firewood makes a wood burner worthy of tax credits.

Oak trees grow along the creek out back, but fall far short of "good oak" status, so we have taken to purchasing dried oak by the truck load – six cords at a crack. Mix hardwoods like maple and elm, along with an abundant supply of aspen, are added to the mix, and together will keep our dwellings toasty warm when winter winds grip the land.

Brother-in-law Mike, a regular weekend visitor, arrives with chainsaw in hand and helps our family put up a winter's supply of fuel for our living room woodstove and a larger outdoor furnace to heat a newly constructed kennel building. With saws, trailers and strong backs we cut, haul and stack our biosolid investment in woodsheds.

On the job of making wood, Leopold continued, "There is an allegory for historians in the diverse functions of saw, wedge and axe. The saw works only across the years – one by one, in sequence. The wedge, on the other hand, yields a collective view of all the years at once. The axe functions only at an angle diagonal to the years – the three tools are requisite to good oak, and to good history."

So, on occasion, we examine our cut wood and count the annual rings. Not much history to be found in the cross-section of a twelve-inch elm, life cut short by Dutch disease. Or a short-lived aspen, which at thirty years old is considered past its prime. The birch and maple that were felled alongside the aspen make room for a new generation of trees that sprout from the stumps and roots of their parents. But short-lived as they are, they reflect the history of our time on this land we call home along the creek. And opposed to fossil fuels, they become a source of energy to heat our buildings.

That makes these words from Leopold hit close to home as we sit by our woodstove, "These things I ponder as the kettle sings, and the good oak burns to red coals on white ashes."

Annually, at the beginning of March, Wisconsin celebrates the life and times of Aldo Leopold on a very special weekend dedicated forever to his legacy. Our inheritance is his words – inspirational thoughts which he left in trust to us all – on nature, conservation and the concept of a land ethic.

His classic work, *A Sand County Almanac* – first published in 1949 – contains a series of essays describing time spent at a weekend retreat from his home and work in Madison. The family "shack" and a worn-out farm, located along the Wisconsin River, became the setting for his beautifully motivated prose. Beyond the seasonal shack essays, he reflected on over forty years of conservation related experiences and finished with a series of philosophical questions that concluded in a land ethic. The final product took him twelve years to write – its impact felt across the globe – with over two million copies printed and translated into nine languages.

Leopold observed "a drama in every bush"…and noted "stories available to any person with ears to hear and eyes to see." He was a wordsmith and a poet, a hunter and an ornithologist, a scholar and a teacher. It was Leopold's lifelong quest to bring people and nature together.

Connecting people with the outdoor world, Leopold truly believed that conservation was "a state of harmony between man and land". It was not simply restoring and protecting land – it was about improving people and changing a culture. To this insightful man, it was more about the banker, the plumber, the farmer, the voter and the consumer. Then and only then, he concluded, will the problems disappear when folks are connected to the land. "Once you learn to read the land, I have no fear of what you will do to it, or with it."

He ended the *Almanac* with the concept of a land ethic – a product of social evolution and man's relationship, or lack of, to land and to the animals and plants which grow upon it. Unfortunately, he notes, man had lost his relation to the land. To most people, "It is the space between cities on which crops grow".

Leopold felt that if we quit thinking about land-use in a purely economic sense and balance what's ethically and economically right – our educational and economic system might head towards a more conscious use of the land. Leopold declared, "A thing is right when it tends to preserve the integrity, stability, and beauty of the biotic community. It is wrong when it tends otherwise."

More than sixty years ago, Leopold penned the following words while introducing *A Sand County Almanac*; "When we see land as a community to which we belong, we may begin to use it with love and respect."

Sixty years later – his words still ring true.

*****

There's a little cabin on the Wisconsin River that's nestled in the woods ninety-one miles downstream from our place. As far as cabins go, it's not much – in fact, it originally housed livestock and fowl – and later became a remodeled weekend refuge for a very special family. Affectionately called "the shack", it was also the focal point of a place that inspired one of our nation's greatest thinkers and wordsmiths.

The year was 1935 and the family sought to rebuild not only the shack, but also the worn-out sand farm that lied along the banks of the river. In the process and over the course of many years – they refashioned the shack and healed the land as a man named Aldo Leopold crafted a masterpiece manuscript that later became *A Sand County Almanac*. More than two million copies have been sold since it was first published posthumously in 1949.

"Like winds and sunsets, wild things were taken for granted until progress began to do away with them. Now we face the question whether a still higher 'standard of living' is worth its cost in things

natural, wild, and free. " Those words in the book's forward and the ones that follow, take the reader on a voyage through the mind of a man that viewed the natural world in four dimensions – far beyond a normal vision. His questions and conclusions on conservation and land ethics have stood the test of time and ultimately became a large part of the modern environmental movement. He was truly a man for all seasons.

Leopold was a hunter and a conservationist, a wordsmith and a poet, a scholar and an artist. His legacy is his words and the people he's influenced – and to this day, his *Almanac* impacts a new generation. Seven years ago, on March 4th, the citizens of Lodi, Wisconsin gathered together and read Leopold's *Almanac* aloud, cover to cover. That event led to the 2004 proclamation by Governor James Doyle, designating the first weekend in March each year as Aldo Leopold Weekend in the state of Wisconsin.

Born in Burlington, Iowa on the banks of the Mississippi River, Leopold began his career with the US Forest Service in the southwestern part of the country – eventually returning to the Midwest as a professor of wildlife management at the University of Wisconsin – Madison. He helped establish and eventually served on the Wisconsin Conservation Commission. There he became deeply involved in deer management issues and led the fight to establish the first doe season. But it was his role as professor, his insatiable desire to write and weekends at the shack that led him to put pencil to paper and create the *Almanac*. His words, like the select following thoughts, have stood the test of time and play like a favorite melody when read aloud.

"These things I ponder as the kettle sings, and the good oak burns to red coals on white ashes...A March morning is only as drab as he who walks in it without a glance skyward, ear cocked for geese...They wind the oxbows of the river, cutting low over the gunless points and islands, and gabbling to each sandbar as to a long lost friend…It is at this moment of each year that I wish I were a muskrat, eye-deep in the marsh."

So, do yourself a favor and enjoy the words of this great man, explore his thoughts about the seasons and travel with him in the Almanac as he travels once around the sun.

*****

Sometimes individuals emerge larger than life long after they are gone. At times, that distinction unfolds during their lifetime.

The year was 1899. A young boy of twelve explored the river bottoms of the Mississippi, gleaning the wonders of nature and hunting with his father Carl. With a talent for drawing, an insatiable appetite for reading and an urge to study birds, mammals and the habitat in which they lived, young Aldo Leopold was on a path towards greatness.

The years passed and then it was 1909. The young boy was now a young man and worked for the Forest Service in New Mexico – where rangers were paid to timber cruise, enforce state game laws and kill predators. Early in his career, Leopold was on reconnaissance with a member of his crew when they noticed an older female wolf and her grown pups. "In those days, we had never heard of passing up a chance to kill a wolf," and concluded that "fewer wolves meant more deer, that no wolves meant hunters' paradise." They reached the old wolf just "in time to watch a fierce green fire dying in her eyes."

That was one of many defining moments for a man that later, in 1933, accepted a position with the University of Wisconsin as Professor of Game Management – the first such instructor in the country. In 1948, Aldo Leopold penned the classic "A Sand County Almanac" – forever defining the scope and depth of the man and as they say, the rest is history.

Fast forward to the year 2011, and we find his poetic words and land ethic message still resonating across the country and beyond our borders. His "green fire" moment now bears the name of a feature length, high definition documentary film *Green Fire: Aldo Leopold and a Land Ethic for Our Time* – produced in partnership between the Aldo Leopold Foundation (ALF), the U.S. Forest Service and the Center for Humans and Nature.

"Aldo Leopold's legacy lives on today in the work of people and organizations across the nation and around the world," said ALF Executive Director Buddy Huffaker. "What is exciting about *Green Fire* is that it is more than just a documentary about Aldo Leopold; it also explores the influence his ideas have had in shaping the conservation movement as we know it today by highlighting some really inspiring people and organizations doing great work to connect people and the natural world in ways that even Leopold might not have imagined."

OF DOVES AND CARDINALS

I stare out the kitchen window and ponder – why in the world do the doves at our feeding station remain here for the winter while the majority of their cousins bask in the southern sun? Why, oh why, do a select few from the autumn flock stay north?

Did you ever wonder why?

The birdwatcher may speculate while simply enjoying the view. The ornithologist explains the science behind migratory pull – caused by the seasonal change in day length, temperature and an ultimate need for food, shelter and water. The philosopher smiles and reflects on the symbolism and stark comparisons between man and beast.

Homo sapiens have adapted to northern climates by adjusting the thermostat, adding insulation and wearing thermal underwear. Those that did not, settled farther south and having less resolve for cold, dealt with the heat. Most of their feathered counterparts simply turned to migration and stayed either one wing beat ahead, or behind the snow line.

Doves, I dare say, are a common sight on the frozen landscape this winter. This year's Audubon Christmas bird count document-ed a healthy mourning dove population in our state – with hun-dreds of birds counted – north and south. Their numbers ranked in the top ten at most locations. Our winter flock of doves numbers twelve. While that is only half the number residing near neighbor Grace's place along the river, it is more than I recall in recent past. We offer a never-ending supply of sunflower seeds, a heated birdbath and a grove of sheltering white pines across the road – consequently providing food, shelter and water.

Perhaps I have answered my own question. Without a handout, those doves might not spend the harshest time of the year in our township, or neighboring cities. A drive down the nearby county trunk highway reveals flock after flock – nine times out of ten near country homes and farmsteads – while in town, bird feeders and doves likely outnumber stop signs and gas stations.

On this, the day of Valentine, it only seems fitting that we speak of doves. English poet and philosopher Geoffrey Chaucer, who was first to associate Valentine's Day with romantic love, coined the term love bird and called today the date when every bird comes to choose his mate. Later, poet Alfred Lord Tennyson penned the verse "In the spring a livelier iris changes on the burnished dove; In the spring a young man's fancy lightly turns to thoughts of love."

But it was Chaucer that started the tradition of Valentine's Day – originally celebrated in early May – when he composed the poem, "The Parliament of Fowls" which literally means "the meeting of birds" – a time when all birds chose their mates. After Chaucer's death in 1400, the celebration of Valentine was pushed back to February, when the first song birds traditionally warbled in England after a long winter.

Spring seems a long way off – with snow piled high and temperatures below normal, but the sight of our flock of doves at the feeding station and the fact that they decided to spend the winter at our side, makes the wait a bit more tolerable.

*****

If I were a bird, I'd fancy myself a cardinal. Like no other, the male of this species displays optimism, cheer and utter vocal determination – bidding winter farewell and ringing in spring with color and flare.

As I hauled water to the horses the other day, our resident male cardinal was greeting all that would care to listen. The thermometer read zero, yet high atop our tallest backyard aspen he welcomed the warmth of the sun and things to come. Nothing the weatherman can say, or the Farmer's Almanac can predict competes with the song of the male cardinal on a late winter morning.

Up and down the river valley – in town and out about the countryside – a cadre of these red birds are welcoming sunshine and warm winds – both signs of winter's demise. Coming out of the winter months plump and sassy, after freeloading at an overstocked feeder, our bird's doctor would recommend exercise and diet – something that will surely come as spring courtship and breeding activity begins.

The vocal abilities of the male cardinal serve several purposes. In late winter and early spring, he sounds off, marking and defending his territory against other males. He will whistle, loud and clear from an elevated perch and defend his territory. Before nesting, he will harmonize with his mate as they prepare for another generation. When danger lurks, he will give a warning alarm call to the female and their chicks.

Did you ever wonder why this bird stands out in the avian crowd? The vibrant color of the male is a result of organic red pigments found in their diet. Sunflower seeds are a good source of these pigments and scientists have determined that the Northern Cardinal males possess the ability to convert these pigments into plumage of a different color than the ingested pigment. That might explain why our doves, consuming the same food remain gray-brown.

No one creature rings in the season with more enthusiasm than a cardinal and no one person described the coming of spring more eloquently than Aldo Leopold. "One swallow does not make a summer, but one skein of geese, cleaving the murk of a March thaw, is the spring. A cardinal, whistling spring to a thaw but later finding himself mistaken, can retrieve his error by resuming his winter silence."

A BIRD DOG FOR BABY SPRAEFKE

There is a special place tucked in the north woods, nestled in aspen and alders, where a country church once stood with pride. It burnt to the ground in 1948 and today, all that indicates its existence are a pair of white crosses – the smaller of the two marking a single grave site of an unnamed newborn that died in 1937. Not long ago, the setting took on new meaning. And that story, as told by my good friend Rich, includes a bird dog named Ranger.

"Legend has it that the child in the grave is a daughter of William Spraefke, aka Whiskey Bill. Not sure if that is true, but the road near the grave was once named Spraefke Road and has since been renamed Whiskey Bill Road. I know there was a man named William Spraefke that lived in the woods off that road at that time. So, it all makes some sense." And according to Rich, "The two crosses are about 30 yards north of Whiskey Bill Road and are nestled in mature aspen with an understory of some alder, a thorn apple thicket and some scattered balsam. You really can't see any remnants of the church or foundation."

Fourteen years ago, Rich and his family packed their truck and experienced 140 miles of "white knuckle driving" through "a January blizzard that we had no business going out in" to pick up an 8-week-old pointer puppy of English decent. They made it home safe and sound – and welcomed "a friend and companion that enriched the lives of our family." But the thing that intrigued

156

Rich the most was "the way he looked into my eyes – literally for hours and hours over his lifetime. What was he thinking?"

Ranger was well travelled – including multiple trips to Montana, North and South Dakota and of course, throughout Wisconsin. Rich recalls many highlights – 14 years of memories. Like in North Dakota, during his first fall and witnessed by friends, including yours truly, "When my pride and joy ran over a big hill and disappeared chasing a large whitetailed buck." And 1998 – 2000, "three years of the best ruffed grouse hunting I've ever had – with the dog that all three sons shot their first birds over. He was in the prime of his life." Or later, the time he became lost pheasant hunting in South Dakota for 45 minutes, and "we found him on point – pointing a rooster near the exact spot we last saw him."

This past fall in Montana, during the twilight of Ranger's life, "the old boy nailed a covey of Hungarian partridge at the end of a shelterbelt on an abandoned homestead, and then proceeded to find singles for me and the rest of our party."

On his last night, he slept with Rich's 18-year-old son Corey, a young man who will leave for the Marines next spring. "Bullet proof and full of macho; sleeping on the floor with an old bird dog, no doubt sharing memories, smiles and tears."

Rich buried Ranger near Whiskey Bill's infant daughter. "So, in my mind I have taken him where there are plenty of grouse and have given the best bird dog I've ever owned to a child that never had a dog."

Rest in peace, buddy.

For nearly three decades, **Ken M. Blomberg** has written a popular outdoor column, "Up the Creek," which has been published in several central Wisconsin newspapers. It currently appears weekly in the *Portage County Gazette* and bi-monthly in the Wisconsin Farm Bureau Federation's *Rural Route* magazine. His freelance articles have appeared in many state and national magazines. Some such magazines include *Field & Stream*, *Fur, Fish & Game*, *Pointing Dog Journal*, *Wing & Shot*, *Ruffed Grouse Society Magazine*, *Bird Dog News*, *Wisconsin Sportsman*, *Badger Sportsman*, and *Woods and Waters*. A 1976 graduate of the University of Wisconsin in Stevens Point (UWSP) with a degree in Resource Management and past Executive Director of the Wisconsin Rural Water Association, Ken is now retired, owns a dog kennel near Junction City, WI and writes full-time.

www.ingramcontent.com/pod-product-compliance
Lightning Source LLC
Chambersburg PA
CBHW050850180626
46814CB00007B/2706